CHE GUEVARA SPEAKS

CHE GUEVARA SPEAKS

PATHFINDER
New York London Montreal Sydney

ISBN 978-0-87348-910-2
Library of Congress Catalog Card Number 67-31739
Manufactured in the United States of America

First edition, 1967
Second edition, 2000
Eighth printing, 2011

Cover design: Eva Braiman
Cover photo: United Nations

"A New Old Interview" is reproduced by permission of
Hispanic American Historical Review.

Pathfinder
www.pathfinderpress.com
E-mail: pathfinder@pathfinderpress.com

Contents

Publisher's note to the second edition

Che Guevara Speaks was published in December 1967, two months after Guevara's death. At the time, it was the first collection of Guevara's writings and speeches published in English. Pathfinder has kept it in print for over three decades.

Since then, a number of other books and pamphlets containing speeches and writings by Guevara have been published by Pathfinder, including *Episodes of the Cuban Revolutionary War, Socialism and Man in Cuba, Che Guevara and the Cuban Revolution, To Speak the Truth, The Bolivian Diary of Ernesto Che Guevara,* and *Che Guevara Talks to Young People.* In producing these works, a painstaking effort was made to provide faithful translations, conveying as fully as possible the political message, literary style, and sense of humor of the author.

When *Che Guevara Speaks* was prepared in the fall of 1967, the Spanish texts available were sometimes incomplete and translations more rough and ready than desirable. These deficiencies were a product of the revolutionary times and the efforts they called forth, not an expression of deliberate carelessness.

For this new edition, Pathfinder has corrected and revised the translations, bringing each one up to the standards our readers deserve. The book has also been newly typeset in modern, more readable type, and has been given a new cover. No other changes have been made, either to the selection or the annotation.

In preparing this second edition, we have sought to preserve what *Che Guevara Speaks* has been for over three decades, as stated in Joseph Hansen's 1967 preface: "a faithful reflection of Che as he was, or, better, as he developed."

JANUARY 2000

Preface

The international sensation caused by the death of Ernesto "Che" Guevara and the dramatic circumstances of the last battles in which he participated have somewhat obscured the true significance of the courageous guerrilla leader as a political figure.

To the older generation, bound up in the past and little able to orient or even to look toward the future, Guevara appears a hopeless romantic, a Don Quixote, an incomprehensible figure driven perhaps by some suicidal impulse.

The youth see him better. To them he appears an admirable example of that complete commitment, that absolute dedication to the advancement of mankind which they instinctively feel represents the highest and noblest attainment an individual can achieve. The vanguard youth are therefore taking Che as their own; he will live for a long time to come in helping to shape the aspirations and goals of the new generation on whom the hope of the world rests.

Yet this says little about the political meaning of Che's rise to world prominence. Something bigger even than Che is involved—the Cuban revolution and its contribution toward solving the most crucial single problem facing humanity: the construction of a leadership capable of guiding the way out of an economic order reeking in every pore with corruption, filth, and blood.

Like many in previous generations, the young people who led the Cuban revolution saw the poverty, the hunger, the abysmal conditions of life, the oppression, making a hell of their country. They also saw how senseless this was and how modern industry and science could change it from top to bottom. Like previous generations they found the contrast between what is and what could be absolutely intolerable. And like many who had preceded them, they saw that, in view of the role of the oligarchy and its imperialist backers, revolution offered the only possible way of ending the insufferable present and opening up a new perspective.

But unlike the majority of those in the immediately preceding decades, they depended on their own judgment, their own initiative, and their own independent efforts to achieve what they sought. They did not fall into either of two very common traps. They did not rely for leadership on the so-called progressive sector of the national bourgeoisie of their own country or on the ossified bureaucracy running the Communist Party.

This was one of the most significant aspects of the Cuban revolution. It provided the main key to success, for it made it possible to outflank the Communist Party, which had stood as the major obstacle to a successful revolution in Cuba since the establishment of the Blas Roca leadership with its policy of "peaceful coexistence" and even collaboration with the Batista dictatorship and the Roosevelt administration.

To Che Guevara, along with Fidel Castro, belongs the credit for hewing to this course of action no matter what the consequences. These leaders and the team they built appeared on the scene, evidently as forerunners of a great new development in world politics—the rise of a generation of revolutionary fighters disinclined to accept either Moscow or Peking or any similar center as a kind of Vatican that in practice serves to stultify both revolutionary theory and practice.

Thus from a political point of view, the major interest in Che Guevara's development is the line of thought and action that enabled him to grow from a petty-bourgeois rebel into an effective leader, committed to the socialist goal, whose outlook converged more and more with the classical revolutionary Marxist tradition that stood behind the October 1917 Russian revolution.

How did Che develop from an idealistic student, inclined to adventurism, into a figure capable of leading a revolution? This question will undoubtedly occupy many students of the revolutionary process today. The raw material required for a rounded answer will be found in Che's deeds, in the memoirs of his friends and comrades, and in his own writings.

The present collection represents an essential part of that record. It consists of speeches, articles, interviews, letters, beginning in 1959 and ending a few months before Che was murdered by the military dictatorship in Bolivia. In selecting the material, the editors have sought to make it representative in order to provide a faithful reflection of Che as he was, or, better, as he developed. To know Che's actual views, including errors in estimation or judgment, is a prerequisite to drawing valid conclusions about his course.

If the collection serves to bring a better appreciation of Che, not just as a model and an example—important as this is—but as a representative of a new type destined to become more and more numerous, a *revolutionist of action*, this book will have proved its value. Che, one may believe, would have accepted this as a worthwhile use of what he wrote and said and did.

Joseph Hansen

Ernesto Che Guevara

Ernesto "Che" Guevara was born in Rosario, Argentina, on June 14, 1928. Both before and after graduating from medical school in 1953, he traveled extensively throughout Latin America. While living in Guatemala in 1954, he became involved in political struggle, opposing the CIA's attempts to overthrow the government of Jacobo Arbenz. Following the ouster of Arbenz, Guevara escaped to Mexico. There, in the summer of 1955, he was selected by Fidel Castro as the third confirmed member of the expeditionary force being organized by the Cuban July 26 Movement to overthrow dictator Fulgencio Batista.

In late November 1956 the eighty-two expeditionaries, including Castro and Guevara, set sail from Tuxpan, Mexico, aboard the yacht *Granma*. The rebel forces landed on Cuba's southeastern coast in Oriente province on December 2 to begin the revolutionary war from the Sierra Maestra mountains in the eastern part of the island. Originally the troop doctor, Guevara was named commander of the second Rebel Army column (Column no. 4) in July 1957. At the end of August 1958 he led Column no. 8 toward Las Villas province in central Cuba. The Las Villas campaign culminated in the capture of Santa Clara, Cuba's third-largest city, and helped seal the fate of the dictatorship.

Following Batista's fall on January 1, 1959, Guevara carried a number of responsibilities in the new revolutionary government, including president of the National Bank and minister of industry, while continuing his duties as an officer in the armed forces. He frequently represented Cuba internationally, including at the United Nations and in other world forums. As a leader of the July 26 Movement, he helped bring about the political regroupment that led to the founding of the Communist Party of Cuba in October 1965.

Guevara resigned his government and party posts, including his military commission and responsibilities, in early 1965 and left Cuba in order to return to South America to help advance the anti-imperialist and anticapitalist struggles that were sharpening in several countries. Along with a number of volunteers who would later join him in Bolivia, Guevara went first to the Congo where he aided the anti-imperialist movement founded by Patrice Lumumba. From November 1966 to October 1967 he led a guerrilla movement in Bolivia against that country's military dictatorship. Wounded and captured by the Bolivian army in a CIA-organized operation on October 8, 1967, he was murdered the following day.

A new old interview

Two Chinese Communist journalists, K'ung Mai and Ping An, interviewed Che Guevara at his home on April 18, 1959, or, as they put it on "the 108th evening after the victory of the revolution." Though Peking radio and the New China News Agency in London gave summaries and a few direct quotations from it, the interview was not reported in any of Peking's three leading newspapers. It was, however, published in full in the lesser-known journal *Shih-chieh Chih-shih* (World Knowledge) of June 5, 1959. This neglected interview apparently never appeared in Cuba, nor was it translated from the Chinese into any other language until William E. Ratliff published a complete English translation, thoroughly documented and annotated, in the *Hispanic American Historical Review* of August 1966.

The Agrarian reform, which Guevara speaks about in the future tense, became law on May 17, 1959, i.e., in the interval between the granting of the interview and its publication in China.

The excerpts below are from Ratliff's translation.

REPORTER: Will you please tell us how Cuba achieved her revolutionary victory?

GUEVARA: Certainly. Let us begin at the time I joined the 26th of July Movement in Mexico. Before the dangerous crossing on the *Granma* the views on society of the members of this organization were very different. I remember, in a frank discussion within our family in Mexico, I suggested we ought to propose a revolutionary program to the Cuban people. I have never forgotten how one of the participants in the attack on the Moncada army camp responded at that time. He said to me: "Our action is very simple. What we want to do is to initiate a coup d'état. Batista pulled off a coup and in only one morning took over the government. We must make another coup and expel him from power. . . . Batista has made a hundred concessions to the Americans, and we will make one hundred and one." At that time I argued with him, saying that we had to make a coup on the basis of principle and yet at the same time understand clearly what we would do after taking over the government. That was the thinking of a member of the first stage of the 26th of July Movement. Those who held the same view and did not change left our revolutionary movement later and adopted another path.

From that time on, the small organization that later made the crossing on the *Granma* encountered repeated difficulties. Besides the never-ending suppression by the Mexican authorities, there was also a series of internal problems, like those people who were adventurous in the beginning but later used this pretext and that to break away from the military expedition. Finally at the time of the crossing on the *Granma* there remained only eighty-two men in the organization.

The adventurous thought of that time was the first and only catastrophe encountered within the organization during the process of starting the uprising. We suffered from the blow. But we gathered together again in the Sierra Maestra. For many months the manner of our life in the mountains was most irregular. We climbed from one mountain peak to another, in a drought, without a drop of water. Merely to survive was extremely difficult.

The peasants who had to endure the persecution of Batista's military units gradually began to change their attitude toward us. They fled to us for refuge to participate in our guerrilla units. In this way our rank and file changed from city people to peasants. At that same time, as the peasants began to participate in the armed struggle for freedom of rights and social justice, we put forth a correct slogan—land reform. This slogan mobilized the oppressed Cuban masses to come forward and fight to seize the land. From this time on the first great social plan was determined, and it later became the banner and primary spearhead of our movement.

It was at just this time that a tragedy occurred in Santiago de Cuba; our comrade Frank País was killed. This produced a turning point in our revolutionary movement. The enraged people of Santiago on their own poured into the streets and called forth the first politically oriented general strike. Even though the strike did not have a leader, it paralyzed the whole of Oriente province. The dictatorial government suppressed the incident. This movement, however, caused us to understand that working class participation in the struggle to achieve freedom was absolutely essential! We then began to carry out secret work among the workers, in preparation for another general strike, to help the Rebel Army seize the government.

The victorious and bold secret activities of the Rebel Army shook the whole country; all of the people were stirred up, leading to the general strike on April 9 last year. But the strike failed because of a lack of contact between the leaders and the working masses. Experience taught the leaders of the 26th of July Movement a valuable truth: the revolution must not belong to this or that specific clique—it must be the undertaking of the whole body of the Cuban people. This conclusion inspired the members of the movement to work their hardest, both on the plains and in the mountains.

At this time we began to educate our forces in revolutionary theory and doctrine. This all showed that the rebel movement had already grown and was even beginning to achieve political maturity. . . .

Every person in the Rebel Army remembered his basic duties in the Sierra Maestra and other areas: to improve the status of the peasants, to participate in the struggle to seize land, and to build schools. Agrarian law was tried for the first time; using revolutionary methods we confiscated the extensive possessions of the officials of the dictatorial government and distributed to the peasants all of the state-held land in the area. At this time there rose up a peasant movement, closely connected to the land, with land reform as its banner. . . .

To carry out thoroughly the law providing for the abolition of the latifundia system will be the concern of the peasant masses themselves. The present state constitution provides for mandatory monetary compensation whenever land is taken away, and land reform under it will be both sluggish and difficult. Now after the victory of the revolution, the peasants who have achieved their freedom must rise up in collective action and democratically demand the abolition of the latifundia system and the carrying out of a true and extensive land reform.

REPORTER: What problems does the Cuban revolution now face, and what are its current responsibilities?

GUEVARA: The first difficulty is that our new actions must be engaged in on the old foundations. Cuba's antipeople regime and army are already destroyed, but the dictatorial social system and economic foundations have not yet been abolished. Some of the old people are still working within the national structure. In order to protect the fruits of the revolutionary victory and to enable the unending development of the revolution we need to take another step forward in our work to rectify and strengthen the government. Second, what the new government took over was a rundown mess. When Batista fled he cleaned out the national treasury, leaving serious difficulties in the national finances. . . . Third, Cuba's land system is one in which *latifundistas* hold large amounts of land, while at the same time many people are unemployed. . . . Fourth, there is still racial discrimination in our society which is not beneficial to efforts to achieve the internal unification of the people. Fifth, our house rents are the highest in the world; a family frequently has to pay over a third of its income for rent. To sum up, the reform of the foundations of the economy of the Cuban society is very difficult and will take a long time.

In establishing the order of society and in democratizing the national life, the new government has adopted many positive measures. We have exerted great effort to restore the national economy. For example, the government has passed a law lowering rents by fifty percent. Yesterday a law regulating beaches was passed to cancel the privileges of a small number of people who occupy the land and the seashores. . . .

Most important is the land reform law, which will soon be promulgated. Moreover, we will found a National Land Reform Institute. Our land reform here is not yet very penetrating; it is not as thorough as the one in China. Yet it must be considered the most progressive in Latin America. . . .

REPORTER: How will Cuba struggle against domestic and foreign reactionary enemies? What are the prospects of the revolution?

GUEVARA: The Cuban revolution is not a class revolution, but a liberation movement that has overthrown a dictatorial, tyrannical government. The people detested the American-supported Batista dictatorial government from the bottoms of their hearts and so rose up and overthrew it. The revolutionary government has received the broad support of all strata of people because its economic measures have taken care of the requirements of all and have gradually improved the livelihood of the people. The only enemies remaining in the country are the *latifundistas* and the reactionary bourgeoisie. They oppose the land reform that goes against their own interests. These internal reactionary forces may get in league with the developing provocations of the foreign reactionary forces and attack the revolutionary government.

The only foreign enemies who oppose the Cuban revolution are the people who monopolize capital and who have representatives in the United States State Department. The victory and continuous development of the Cuban revolution has caused these people to panic. They do not willingly accept defeat and are doing everything possible to maintain their control over the Cuban government and economy and to block the great influence of the Cuban revolution on the people's struggles in the other Latin American countries. . . .

Our revolution has set an example for every other country in Latin America. The experience and lessons of our revolution have caused the mere talk of the coffee houses to be dispersed like smoke. We have proved that an uprising can begin even when there is only a small group of fearless men with a resolute will; that it is only necessary to gain the support of the people who can then compete with, and in the end defeat, the regular disciplined army of the government. It is also necessary to carry out a land reform. This is another experience that our Latin American brothers ought to absorb. On the economic front and in agricultural structure they are at the same stage as we are.

The present indications are very clear that they are now preparing to intervene in Cuba and destroy the Cuban revolution. The evil foreign enemies have an old method. First they begin a political offensive, propagandizing widely and saying that the Cuban people oppose Communism. These false democratic leaders say that the United States cannot allow a Communist country on its coastline. At the same time they intensify their economic attack and cause Cuba to fall into economic difficulties. Later they will look for a pretext to create some kind of dispute and then utilize certain international organizations they control to carry out intervention against the Cuban people. We do not have to fear an attack from some small neighboring dictatorial country, but from a certain large country, using certain international organizations and a certain kind of pretext in order to intervene and undermine the Cuban revolution. . . .

Fidel's trip to New York

The following excerpt is from a speech by Guevara on September 17, 1960.

The more that the imperialist forces (who act from without) and the reactionary forces (who are their natural allies from within) increase their pressure against the Cuban revolution, the more it will deepen, responding to the voice of the people and adopting more and more drastic measures. . . . The ink is still fresh in our *Gazette,* with which we have just finished printing Resolution no. 2, nationalizing the U.S. banks.

And while it is still fresh, compañero Fidel is packing his knapsack to go to New York. I use the words "packing his knapsack," first of all, because we're dealing with a combat assignment and it therefore merits such a literary figure of speech. But he is also packing his knapsack because the U.S. imperialists, submerged in barbarism, wish to deprive him even of the right that all members of the United Nations have to live in the place where the United Nations is located, in the United States of America. And Fidel Castro has clearly announced that he is taking his knapsack and his hammock with a nylon awning, and we should not be surprised if tomorrow we see a photo of our delegation slinging its hammocks in Central Park, in the most barbaric nation on earth.

And that's logical. We slung our hammocks up in the mountains when Cuba was submerged in barbarism and we were fighting for her liberation. Therefore we can sling our hammocks today in the center of that barbaric civilization, to defend the right of all peoples to achieve their liberty, their total economic independence, and their right to freely chose whatever path their people decide on.

But Fidel will go preceded by this new measure that will deepen the struggle, a measure that will bring economic problems, but which we have adopted precisely in order to defend our dignity and our right to be free. For many years now imperialism has based its economic power on money, on the banks, and little by little has taken possession of the peoples and twisted their economies, until it has converted these peoples into a simple appendage of the greater economy of the empire.

That is how our potent sugar industry developed; it did not fall from the sky, nor did it develop out of U.S. kindness, but because they dominated the great *sugar mills*, those with the highest productivity. They dominated the entire market and paid us a preferential price. They did so in order that, sheltered by these prices, they could introduce into our country, by means of a law falsely called the law of reciprocity, all the manufactured consumer articles used by the people. Furthermore, they did so under conditions in which the competition of other countries that produced consumer goods was impossible. . . .

But the U.S. way of doing things requires accomplices. They could not, as in the ancient times of the Roman Empire, hurl their legions upon a conquered country and put there a proconsul representing the Empire. They needed a proconsul, but one with special characteristics, outfitted in the modern manner and at times suave of demeanor, but revealing always his imperial essence. And those proconsuls were sometimes ambassadors, sometimes bank presidents, and sometimes the heads of military missions. But they always spoke English.

It was precisely in the dark epoch of the sugar depression that the task of the banks was very important, since all depressions are always felt by the mass of the people. Depressions are when the great monopolies see their profits increased and when they consolidate their economic empire, absorbing all the small ones, all the sardines in this sea of economic struggle. Thus in that epoch the U.S. banks had an important task. It was the task of foreclosing for debts, according to the laws of the country, on all those who could not resist the force of the depression; and they rapidly consolidated their empires. Always they belong to the vanguard of the great financial groups that vie for power in the United States.

They belong to the Rockefellers, the Mellons, the Morgans, and all those who have deployed their tentacles among the three branches that sustain the power of the United States: finance, the army and, as a simple kid brother, the government. Because the government of the United States represents the financial interests of the United States, as does its army. But these financial interests do not represent the people of the United States; they represent a small group of financiers. They represent the owners of all the big corporations, the owners of money, who also exploit the people of the United States. Clearly they do not exploit them in the same way they exploit us, people of inferior races, the mestizos of America, Africa, and Asia, for we have not had the good fortune of being born from blond, Anglo-Saxon parents. But they too are exploited and divided; they too are divided into Blacks and whites, men and women, union and nonunion, employed and unemployed. . . .

Because of this it is good to see that the first stage of imperialist division—disunity—has been absolutely conquered here. We no longer need to be ashamed of the color of our skin. We no longer need to fear that because of our sex or social status we will not get a job, or else get one at lower pay. When the working class is united, when the peasants of the country are united, the first step toward definitive liberation is taken. Because the old, the very old, imperial maxim "divide and conquer" remains, today as yesterday, the basis of imperialist strategy.

Ideology of the Cuban revolution

Guevara wrote "Notes for the Study of the Ideology of the Cuban Revolution" for the October 8, 1960, issue of *Verde Olivo*, the magazine of Cuba's armed forces.

This is a unique revolution, which for some does not fit in with one of the most orthodox premises of the revolutionary movement, expressed by Lenin: "Without revolutionary theory there can be no revolutionary movement." It should be said that revolutionary theory, as the expression of a social truth, stands above any particular presentation of it. In other words, one can make a revolution if historical reality is interpreted correctly and if the forces involved are utilized correctly, even without knowing theory.

In every revolution there is always involvement by people from very different tendencies who, nevertheless, come to agreement on action and on the most immediate objectives. It is clear that if the leaders have adequate theoretical knowledge prior to taking action, many errors can be avoided, as long as the adopted theory corresponds to reality.

The principal actors of this revolution had no coherent viewpoint. But it cannot be said that they were ignorant of the various concepts of history, society, economics, and revolution being discussed in the world today. A profound knowledge of reality, a close relationship with the people, the firmness of the objective being sought, and the experience of revolutionary practice gave those leaders the opportunity to form a more complete theoretical conception.

The foregoing should be considered an introduction to the explanation of this curious phenomenon that has intrigued the entire world: the Cuban revolution. How and why did a group of men, cut to ribbons by an army enormously superior in technique and equipment, manage first to survive, then to become strong, later to become stronger than the enemy in the battle zones, move into new combat zones still later, and finally defeat that enemy in pitched battles even though their troops were still vastly outnumbered? This is a deed that deserves to be studied in the history of the contemporary world.

Naturally we, who often do not show due concern for theory, will not proceed today to expound the truth of the Cuban revolution as if we were its owners. We are simply trying to lay the foundation for being able to interpret this truth. In fact, the Cuban revolution must be separated into two absolutely different stages: that of the armed action up to January 1, 1959; and the political, economic, and social transformations from then on.

Even these two stages deserve further subdivisions. We will not deal with them from the viewpoint of historical exposition, however, but from the viewpoint of the evolution of the revolutionary thinking of its leaders through their contact with the people.

Incidentally, here we must introduce a general attitude toward one of the most controversial terms of the modern world: Marxism. When asked whether or not we are Marxists, our position is the same as that of a physicist when asked if he is a "Newtonian" or of a biologist when asked if he is a "Pasteurian."

There are truths so evident, so much a part of the peoples' knowledge, that it is now useless to debate them. One should be a "Marxist" with the same naturalness with which one is a "Newtonian" in physics or a "Pasteurian" in biology, considering that if new facts bring about new concepts, the latter will never take away that portion of truth possessed by those that have come before. Such is the case, for example, of "Einsteinian" relativity or of Planck's quantum theory in relation to Newton's discoveries. They take absolutely nothing away from the greatness of the learned Englishman. Thanks to Newton, physics was able to advance until it achieved new concepts of space. The learned Englishman was the necessary steppingstone for that.

Obviously, one can point to certain mistakes of Marx, as a thinker and as an investigator of the social doctrines and of the capitalist system in which he lived. We Latin Americans, for example, cannot agree with his interpretation of Bolívar, or with his and Engels's analysis of the Mexicans, which were made accepting as fact even certain theories of race or nationality that are unacceptable today. But the great men who discover brilliant truths live on despite their small faults, and these faults serve only to show us they were human. That is to say, they were human beings who could make mistakes, even given the high level of consciousness achieved by these giants of human thought. This is why we recognize the essential truths of Marxism as part of humanity's body of cultural and scientific knowledge. We accept it with the naturalness of something that requires no further argument.

The advances in social and political science, as in other fields, belong to a long historical process whose links are constantly being connected, added up, bound together, and perfected. In early human history, there existed Chinese, Arab, or Hindu mathematics; today, mathematics has no frontiers. A Greek Pythagoras, an Italian Galileo, an English Newton, a German Gauss, a Russian Lobachevsky, an Einstein, etc., all have a place in the history of the peoples. Similarly, in the field of social and political sciences, a long series of thinkers, from Democritus to Marx, have added their original investigations and accumulated a body of experience and doctrines.

The merit of Marx is that he suddenly produces a qualitative change in the history of social thought. He interprets history, understands its dynamic, foresees the future. But in addition to foreseeing it (by which he would meet his scientific obligation), he expresses a revolutionary concept: it is not enough to interpret the world, it must be transformed. Man ceases to be the slave and instrument of his environment and becomes an architect of his own destiny. At that moment Marx begins to put himself in a position where he becomes the necessary target of all those who have a special interest in maintaining the old—like what happened to Democritus, whose work was burned by Plato himself and his disciples, the ideologues of the Athenian slave-owning aristocracy. Beginning with the revolutionary Marx, a political group is established with concrete ideas, which, based on the giants, Marx and Engels, and developing through successive stages with individuals such as Lenin, Stalin, Mao Tse-tung, and the new Soviet and Chinese rulers, establishes a body of doctrine and, shall we say, examples to follow.

The Cuban revolution takes up Marx at the point where he put aside science to pick up his revolutionary rifle. And it takes him up at that point not in a spirit of revisionism, of struggling against that which came after Marx, of reviving a "pure" Marx, but simply because up to that point Marx, the scientist, standing outside of history, studied and predicted. Afterward, Marx the revolutionary took up the fight as part of history.

We, practical revolutionaries, by initiating our struggle were simply fulfilling laws foreseen by Marx the scientist. And along that road of rebellion, by struggling against the old power structure, by basing ourselves on the people to destroy that structure, and by having the well-being of the people as the foundation of our struggle, we are simply fitting into the predictions of Marx the scientist. That is to say, and it is well to emphasize this once again: the laws of Marxism are present in the events of the Cuban revolution, independently of whether its leaders profess or fully know those laws from a theoretical point of view . . .

Each one of those small historical moments of the guerrilla war framed different social concepts and different appraisals of Cuban reality. They shaped the thinking of the military leaders of the revolution, who in time would also reaffirm their status as political leaders.

Before the landing of the *Granma,* a mentality predominated that, to some degree, might be called subjectivist: blind confidence in a rapid popular explosion, enthusiasm and faith in being able to destroy Batista's might by a swift uprising combined with spontaneous revolutionary strikes, and the subsequent fall of the dictator. . . .

After the landing comes the defeat, the almost total destruction of the forces, their regroupment and formation as a guerrilla force. The small numbers of survivors, survivors with the will to struggle, were characterized by their understanding of the falsehood of the imagined schema of spontaneous outbursts throughout the island. They understood also that the fight would have to be a long one and that it would need to have a large peasant participation. At this point too, the first peasants joined the guerrillas. Also, two clashes were fought, of little importance in terms of the number of combatants, but of great psychological value, since they erased the uneasiness toward the peasants felt by the guerrillas' central group, made up of people from the cities. The peasants, in turn, distrusted the group and, above all, feared barbarous reprisals from the government. Two things were demonstrated at this stage, both very important for these interrelated factors: The peasants saw that the bestialities of the army and all the persecution would not be sufficient to put an end to the guerrillas, but would be capable of wiping out the peasants' homes, crops, and families. So a good solution was to take refuge with the guerrillas, where their lives would be safe. In turn, the guerrilla fighters learned the ever-greater necessity of winning the peasant masses. . . .

[Following the failure of Batista's major assault on the Rebel Army,] the war shows a new characteristic: the relationship of forces turns in favor of the revolution. During a month and a half, two small columns, one of 80 and the other of 140 men, constantly surrounded and harassed by an army that mobilized thousands of soldiers, crossed the plains of Camagüey, arrived at Las Villas, and began the job of cutting the island in two.

At times it may seem strange, or incomprehensible, or even incredible that two columns of such small size—without communications, without transport, without the most elementary arms of modern warfare—could fight well-trained, and above all, well-armed troops. The fundamental thing is the characteristic of each group. The fewer comforts the guerrilla fighter has, the more he is initiated into the rigors of nature, the more he feels at home, the higher his morale, the higher his sense of security. At the same time, under whatever circumstances, the guerrilla has come to put his life on the line, to trust it to the luck of a tossed coin. And in general, whether or not the individual guerrilla lives or dies weighs little in the final outcome of the battle.

The enemy soldier, in the Cuban example that we are

now considering, is the junior partner of the dictator. He is the man who gets the last crumbs left by the next-to-last hanger-on in a long chain that begins on Wall Street and ends with him. He is ready to defend his privileges, but only to the degree that they are important. His salary and his benefits are worth some suffering and some dangers, but they are never worth his life. If that is the price of keeping them, better to give them up, in other words, to retreat from the guerrilla danger.

From these two concepts and these two morales springs the difference that would reach the crisis point on December 31, 1958.

The superiority of the Rebel Army was being established more and more clearly. Furthermore, the arrival of our columns in Las Villas showed the greater popularity of the July 26 Movement compared to all other groups: the Revolutionary Directorate, the Second Front of Las Villas, the Popular Socialist Party, and some small guerrilla forces of the Authentic Organization. In large part this was due to the magnetic personality of its leader, Fidel Castro, but the greater correctness of its revolutionary line was also a factor.

Here ended the insurrection. But the men who arrive in Havana after two years of arduous struggle in the mountains and plains of Oriente, in the plains of Camagüey, and in the mountains, plains, and cities of Las Villas are not the same ideologically as the ones who landed on the beaches of Las Coloradas, or who joined in the first phase of the struggle. Their distrust of the peasant has turned into affection and respect for his virtues. Their total ignorance of life in the countryside has turned into a profound knowledge of the needs of our peasants. Their dabbling with statistics and with theory has been replaced by the firm cement of practice.

With agrarian reform as their banner, the implementation of which begins in the Sierra Maestra, these men come up against imperialism. They know that the agrarian reform is the basis upon which the new Cuba will be built. They know also that the agrarian reform will give land to all the dispossessed, but that it will dispossess its unjust possessors. And they know that the largest of the unjust possessors are also influential men in the State Department or in the government of the United States of America. But they have learned to conquer difficulties with courage, with audacity, and above all, with the support of the people. And they have now seen the future of liberation that awaits us on the other side of our sufferings. . . .

Mobilizing the masses for the invasion

The following is from a speech by Guevara to sugar workers in Santa Clara on March 28, 1961, twenty days before the Bay of Pigs invasion.

. . . We must remind ourselves of this at every moment: that we are in a war, a cold war as they call it. We are in a war where there is no front line, no continuous bombardment, but where the two adversaries—this tiny champion of the Caribbean and the immense imperialist hyena—stand face to face, knowing that one of them is going to end up dead in the fight.

The North Americans are aware—they are well aware, compañeros—that the victory of the Cuban revolution will not be just a simple defeat for the empire, not just another link in the long chain of defeats it's been suffering in its policy of force and oppression against the peoples in recent years. The victory of the Cuban revolution will be a tangible demonstration before all the Americas that the peoples are capable of rising up, that they can proclaim their independence in the very clutches of the monster. It will mean the beginning of the end of colonial domination in Latin America, that is, the beginning of the definitive end of U.S. imperialism.

That is why the imperialists do not resign themselves. That is why this is a struggle to the death. That is why we cannot take a single step backward, because the first time we retreat one step would be the beginning of a long chain for us too. And we would end up the same way as all the traitorous regimes and all the peoples who at a given moment of history were incapable of resisting the drive of the empire.

That is why we must move forward, striking out tirelessly against imperialism. From all over the world we have to learn the lessons presented to us. We must turn Lumumba's murder into a lesson.

The murder of Patrice Lumumba is an example of what the empire does when the struggle against it is carried on in a firm and sustained way. Imperialism must be hit in its snout again and again, and yet again, in an infinite series of blows and counterblows. That is the only way the people can achieve their true independence.

Never a step backward, never a moment of weakness! And every time circumstances might tempt us to think that the situation might be better if we were not fighting the empire, let each of us think of the long chain of tortures and deaths through which the Cuban people had to pass to win their independence. Let all of us think of the eviction of peasants, of the murder of workers, of the strikes broken by the police, of all those manifestations of oppression by a class that has completely disappeared from Cuba. . . . And, let us also understand well how victory is won; victory is won by preparing the people, by enhancing their revolutionary consciousness, by establishing unity, by meeting each and every attempt at aggression with our rifles in hand. That is how it is won. . . .

We must remember something and insist again and again upon it: The victory of the Cuban people can never come solely through outside aid, however adequate and generous it may be, however great and strong the solidarity of all the peoples of the world with us may be. Because even with the wholehearted solidarity of all the people of the world with Patrice Lumumba and the Congolese people, when conditions inside the country went wrong, when the government leaders failed to understand how to strike back mercilessly at imperialism, when they took a step back, they lost the struggle. And they lost it not just for a few years, but for who knows how many years! That was a great setback for all the peoples.

That is what we ourselves must be well aware of, that Cuba's victory lies not in Soviet rockets, not in the solidarity of the socialist world, not in the solidarity of the entire world. Cuba's victory lies in the unity, the work, and the spirit of sacrifice of its people.

Cuban exceptionalism?

The following selection is from Guevara's article "Cuba: Historical Exception or Vanguard in the Struggle against Colonialism?" in the April 9, 1961, issue of *Verde Olivo*, the magazine of Cuba's armed forces.

. . . Some sectors, in good faith or with axes to grind, claim to see [in the Cuban revolution] a series of exceptional origins and features and they artificially inflate the relative importance of these into the decisive factor. They speak of the exceptionalism of the Cuban revolution, in comparison to the course charted by other progressive parties in Latin America. And they conclude from it that the method and the road of the Cuban revolution are unique, and that in other countries of Latin America the historical course of the peoples will be different.

We accept that there were exceptions that gave the Cuban revolution peculiar characteristics. It is a clearly established fact that every revolution has this type of specific factors, but it is no less established that all revolutions follow laws that society is unable to violate. Let us analyze, then, the factors of this purported exceptionalism.

The first, perhaps the most important, the most original exceptional factor, is that terrestrial force called Fidel Castro Ruz, a name that in a few years has attained historic proportions. The future will accord our prime minister's merits their exact place, but to us they appear comparable to those of the greatest historic figures of all Latin America. And what are the exceptional circumstances that surround the personality of Fidel Castro? There are various features of his life and character that make him stand out far above all his compañeros and followers. Fidel is a man of such tremendous personality that he would gain the leadership in whatever movement he participated in. So it has been throughout his career from his student days to the premiership of our country and of the oppressed peoples of Latin America. He has the qualities of a great leader, and added to these are his personal gifts of audacity, strength, courage, and an extraordinary concern to always discern the will of the people. These qualities have brought him to the position of honor and sacrifice that he occupies today. But he has other important qualities, such as his ability to assimilate knowledge and experience in order to understand a situation as a whole without losing sight of the details, his immense faith in the future, and the breadth of his vision to foresee and anticipate events, always seeing farther and better than his compañeros. With these great cardinal qualities, with his capacity to bring people together and unite them, opposing the division that weakens; with his ability to lead the whole people in action; with his infinite love for the people; with his faith in the future and his capacity to foresee it, Fidel Castro did more than anyone else in Cuba to construct from nothing the now-formidable edifice that is the Cuban revolution.

However, no one can assert that Cuba had political and social conditions that were totally different from those in other countries of Latin America, and that the revolution took place precisely because of such a difference. Nor can anyone assert, on the other hand, that Fidel Castro made the revolution despite that difference. Fidel, a great and able leader, led the revolution in Cuba, at the time and in the way he did, by interpreting the profound political upheavals that were preparing the people for the great leap onto the revolutionary road. Also certain conditions existed that were not unique to Cuba, but that will be difficult for other peoples to take advantage of again because imperialism—in contrast to some progressive groups—does indeed learn from its errors.

The one condition that we could describe as exceptional was that U.S. imperialism was disoriented and was never able to accurately gauge the true scope of the Cuban revolution. This helps explain many of the apparent contradictions in the so-called Fourth Estate in the United States. The monopolies, as is habitual in such cases, began to think about a successor to Batista precisely because they knew that the people were dissatisfied and were also looking for a successor to Batista—but along revolutionary paths. What more intelligent and clever stroke therefore, than to get rid of the now unserviceable little dictator and to replace him with "new boys" who could in their turn serve the interests of imperialism very well? The empire gambled on this card from its continental deck for a while, and lost miserably. Prior to the triumph they were suspicious but not afraid of us; rather, with all their experience at this game, which they were accustomed to winning, they played with two decks. On various occasions, emissaries of the State Department, disguised as journalists, came to investigate our rustic revolution, but they never came away with any sense of imminent danger in it. By the time imperialism wanted to react, when the imperialists discovered that the group of inexperienced young men who were marching in triumph through the streets of Havana had a clear awareness of their political duty and an iron determination to carry out that duty, it was already too late. Thus in January 1959, there dawned the first social revolution in the Caribbean and the deepest revolution in the Americas.

We don't believe that it could be considered exceptional that the bourgeoisie, or at least a good part of it, showed itself favorable to the revolutionary war against the tyranny at the same time that it was supporting and promoting movements that looked for negotiated solutions that would permit them to replace the Batista regime with elements disposed to curb the revolution.

Considering the conditions in which the revolutionary war was waged and the complexity of the political tendencies that opposed the tyranny, it was not at all exceptional that some plantation owners adopted a neutral, or at least nonbelligerent, attitude toward the insurrectionary forces. It is understandable that the national bourgeoisie, cowed by imperialism and the tyranny, whose troops sacked small properties and made extortion a daily way of life, felt a certain sympathy when they saw those young rebels from the mountains punish the military arm of imperialism, which is what the mercenary army was.

In this way nonrevolutionary forces did in fact help smooth the road for the advent of revolutionary power.

Going further, we can add as an additional factor of exceptionalism the fact that in most places in Cuba the peasants had been proletarianized by the requirements of big semi-mechanized capitalist agriculture, and had reached a stage of organization that gave them greater class-consciousness. We can admit this. But we should point out, in the interest of truth, that the first zone of operations of the Rebel Army—made up of the survivors of the defeated column that had made the voyage on the *Granma*—was an area inhabited by peasants whose social and cultural roots were different from those of the peasants found in the areas of large-scale semimechanized agriculture in Cuba. In effect, the Sierra Maestra, scene of the first revolutionary column, is a place where peasants struggling barehanded against the plantation system took refuge. They went there seeking to snatch from the state or some voracious plantation owner a new piece of land on which to earn their modest fortune. They had to constantly struggle against the extortion of the soldiers, who were always allied to the plantation owners; and their aspiration extended no farther than a property deed. Concretely, the soldiers who belonged to our first peasant-type guerrilla army came from the part of this social class that shows most aggressively its love for the land and the possession of it; in other words, that shows most perfectly what can be defined as the petty-bourgeois spirit. The peasant fought because he wanted land—for himself, for his children, to manage it, sell it, and get rich by his work.

Despite his petty-bourgeois spirit, the peasant soon learned that he could not satisfy his hunger for the land without breaking up the plantation system. Radical agrarian reform—which is the only kind of reform that could give land to the peasants—clashed directly with the interests of the imperialists, the plantation owners, and the sugar and cattle magnates. The bourgeoisie was afraid to fight those interests. But the proletariat was not afraid to fight them. In this way the very course of the revolution united the workers and peasants. The workers supported the demands against the plantation owners. The poor peasant, rewarded with ownership of the land, loyally supported the revolutionary power and defended it against its imperialist and counterrevolutionary enemies.

In our opinion no additional factors of exceptionalism can be alleged. We have been more than generous in stating them.

Now we shall examine the permanent roots of all social phenomena in Latin America, the contradictions maturing in the womb of present societies, which provoke changes that can attain the magnitude of a revolution like Cuba's.

First in chronological order, though not in the order of importance at present, is latifundism, the plantation system. The plantation system was the foundation of the economic power of the ruling class throughout the entire period that followed the great anticolonialist revolution for liberty of the last century. But that latifundist social class, which is found in all of the countries, generally lags behind the social developments that stir the world. In some places, however, the most alert and clear-sighted section of the latifundist class is aware of the dangers and is changing the type of investment of their capital, at times going in for mechanized agriculture, transferring some of their wealth to industrial investment, or becoming commercial agents of the monopolies. In any case, the first revolution for liberty never destroyed the latifundist foundation that always served as a reactionary force and upheld the principle of servitude on the land. This is a phenomenon common to all the countries of Latin America without exception. It has been underneath all the injustices committed since the era when the King of Spain gave huge grants of land to his most noble *conquistadores*. In the case of Cuba, he left for the natives, Creoles, and mestizos only the *realengos*, that is, the scraps of land falling between the convergence of three circular grants.

In most countries the plantation owners realized they couldn't survive alone and promptly entered into alliance with the monopolies, that is, with the strongest and cruelest oppressor of the Latin American peoples. North American capital arrived on the scene to make the virgin lands bear fruit, so that it could later carry off unnoticed all the funds it had so "generously" given—plus several times the amount originally invested in the "beneficiary" country.

Latin America was a field of interimperialist struggle. The "wars" between Costa Rica and Nicaragua, the separation of Panama from Colombia, the infamy committed against Ecuador in its dispute with Peru, the fight between Paraguay and Bolivia—these are nothing but expressions of the gigantic battle between the world's great monopolistic consortiums, a battle decided almost completely in favor of the U.S. monopolies following World War II. From that point on, the empire devoted itself to strengthening its grip on its colonial possessions and putting in place the best possible structure to prevent the intrusion of old or new competitors from other imperialist countries. All this resulted in a monstrously distorted economy, which has been described by the shamefaced economists of the imperialist system using an innocuous term that reveals the deep pity they feel for us inferior beings. "Poor little Indian" is the term they use for our miserably exploited Indians, persecuted and reduced to utter wretchedness. "Colored" is the term they use for all blacks and mulattos, disinherited and discriminated against—used individually as instruments; used collectively as a means of dividing the working masses in their struggle for a better economic future. For us, the peoples of Latin America, they have another polite and refined term: "underdeveloped."

What is "underdevelopment"?

A dwarf with an enormous head and a swollen chest is "underdeveloped," inasmuch as his weak legs or short arms do not match the rest of his anatomy. He is the product of an abnormal formation that distorted his development. That is really what we are—we, who are politely referred to as "underdeveloped," but in truth are colonial, semicolonial, or dependent countries. We are countries whose economies have been twisted by imperialism, which has abnormally developed in us those branches of industry or agriculture needed to complement its complex economy. "Underdevelopment," or distorted development, brings with it dangerous specialization in raw materials, inherent in which is the threat of hunger for all our peoples. We, the "underdeveloped," are also those with a one-crop agricultural system, with a single product, with a single market. A single product whose uncertain sale depends on a single market that imposes and fixes conditions—that is the great formula for imperialist economic domination. It should be added to the old, but eternally young, Roman slogan: divide and conquer!

Latifundism, then, through its connections with imperialism, completely shapes so-called underdevelopment, whose results are low wages and unemployment. This phenomenon of low wages and unemployment is a vicious cycle that produces ever lower wages and ever more unemployment, as the great contradictions of the system sharpen—constantly at the mercy of the cyclical fluctuations of its own economy. This situation provides the common denominator of all the peoples of the Americas, from the Río Bravo* to the South Pole. This common denominator, which we shall print in capital letters and which serves as the starting point for an analysis by all who think about these social phenomena, is called THE HUNGER OF THE PEOPLE. This hunger consists of a weariness of being oppressed, persecuted, exploited to the limit; a weariness of selling their labor-power at miserable prices day after day (faced with the fear of swelling the enormous mass of unemployed) so that the greatest profit can be wrung from each human body, profits that are later squandered in the orgies of the masters of capital.

We see, then, that there are great and inescapable common denominators in Latin America. We cannot say we were exempt from any of those factors leading to the most terrible and permanent of all: the hunger of the people. Lat-

---

* The Latin American name for the river called the Rio Grande in the United States.

ifundism, whether as a primitive form of exploitation or as a form of capitalist monopoly of the land, adjusts to the new conditions and becomes an ally of imperialism. Imperialism is a form of exploitation at the hands of finance and monopoly capitalism outside its national borders. The aim is to create economic colonialism, euphemistically called "underdevelopment," resulting in low wages, underemployment, unemployment: the hunger of the people. All this used to exist in Cuba. Here, too, there was hunger. The percentage of unemployed here was one of the highest in Latin America. Imperialism was crueler here than in many countries of Latin America. And latifundism here was as strong as in any sister country.

What did we do to free ourselves from the great phenomenon of imperialism with its train of puppet rulers in each country and with mercenary armies to protect the puppets and the whole complex social system of the exploitation of man by man? We applied certain formulas, which on previous occasions we have given out as discoveries of our empirical medicine for the great evils of our beloved Latin America, empirical medicine that soon found its place within scientific truth.

The objective conditions for the struggle are provided by the hunger of the people, their reaction to that hunger, the terror unleashed to crush the people's reaction, and the wave of hatred that the repression creates. Latin America lacked the subjective conditions, the most important of which is awareness of the possibility of victory through violent struggle against the imperialist powers and their internal allies. These conditions were created through armed struggle, which makes clear the need for change (and made it possible to foresee it) and for the defeat and subsequent annihilation of the army by the popular forces *(an absolutely essential condition for every true revolution)*.

Having already shown that these conditions are created

through armed struggle, we must explain once more that such a struggle should be conducted in the countryside. From the countryside a peasant army, pursuing the great objectives for which the peasantry should fight (the first of which is the just distribution of the land), will capture the cities. Basing itself on the ideology of the working class, whose great thinkers discovered the social laws governing us, the peasant class of Latin America will provide the great army of liberation of the future, as it has already done in Cuba. This army created in the countryside, where the subjective conditions keep ripening for the seizure of power, proceeds to take the cities, uniting with the working class and in so doing enriching itself ideologically. It can and must defeat the oppressor army, at first in skirmishes, clashes, surprise attacks; at the end in large battles. By this time the people's army will have grown from a small-scale guerrilla force into a great popular army of liberation. One stage in the consolidation of the revolutionary power, as we indicated above, will be the elimination of the old army. . . .

Cuba's economic plan

The People's University is the name of a television program in Cuba that features lectures and other educational programs. It had been originally inaugurated by Guevara, and on April 30, 1961, though the din of the defeated invasion had barely died down, he appeared on the program to deliver an important speech on the country's economic plans. In the course of the program he utilized charts, maps, and other visual materials.

. . . The fact is that the process of state acquisition of the means of production is following two more or less parallel roads: one is the logical and conscious course toward defined goals by a state whose decrees and laws have nationalized the principal industries; the other is the result of the collective weapons of a defeated class and the political commotions that have continued uninterruptedly these last two years.

There is a series of laws, including some laws administered by the Ministry of the Treasury through the office of its subsecretariat for the Recovery of Property, which at first confiscated ill-gotten wealth—an indiscriminate assortment, both large and small—and at present confiscates the property of individuals committing acts against the security of the state.

So that when the great split occurred in the petty bourgeoisie, one part—more conscious, more ideologically alert, more patriotic, more courageous, possessing no means of production, not even small ones—took the side of the state, the revolution, the people, and set to work to integrate themselves into the revolution. The other part, however, maintained relations of deepening subservience—above all ideologically but often economically—to the bourgeoisie, which was in the process of being defeated. This section began to conspire or to flee abroad. And through this process it left a string of small enterprises that the ministry had to take over in order to provide employment for the workers.

This has been a continuous process. Unfortunately, although we have tried to stem it by offering guarantees, the temptation held out by the U.S. power has proved greater than our pledges. Small industrialists and merchants have sometimes been tempted by the idea of returning as conquerors, other times simply out of fear, other times with the idea of winning a gold braid in the mountains somewhere or in underground work. And they have engaged in conspiratorial activities and been discovered by our immense intelligence service, which is the entire people of Cuba.

As a result then, we receive a gift, by no means a welcome one, of a shed with seven workers, without sanitary facilities, without the slightest mechanization, without the most elementary notion of organization. But these are seven men who must have work because they have to feed their families. Naturally, we take them in as best we can and try to rationalize the industry. . . .

[*Utilizing a chart, Guevara completes his explanation of the set-up and functioning of the Ministry of Industry.*]

All right. We have analyzed perfectly—all right, not perfectly, but within the speaker's limitations—what is an enterprise, the productive part of this organization. The ministry's other function is planning, that is, projecting, forecasting the future. For this, for projecting the future, you must draw up a plan. And this raises the question of what a plan is.

I am not going to elaborate on what a plan is, to say nothing of making theoretical comparisons. We are talking about what a plan is in a socialist country. We can say what the basic preconditions for a plan are.

The first precondition in designing a plan is control over the means of production. The absolute precondition for an economic plan is that the state control the majority of the means of production, and better yet, if possible, all the means of production.

That is, a real economic plan is a centralized state plan based on a socialist conception of the economy. But all this may simply be—and in our case it was—just the first step. We now have control of the means of production. Can we create a plan through control of the means of production alone? It cannot be done. To make a plan you have to have a clear picture of the national reality. That is, you must have firm, precise, meticulous statistical knowledge of all economic factors; and that is the difficulty. Because we in Cuba all know, and all our foreign visitors know, that the basic characteristic of economic colonialism, as it is of capitalism too, is anarchy. So the difficulty is the absence of sound statistical data that would give us a clear picture of the situation.

Throughout the state apparatus, the revolutionary government is actively working to complete this phase, the statistical data-gathering phase, and it's virtually completed. Once we have the statistical knowledge and control over the means of production, we must make certain of the goals we aim to achieve. You have to have a clear idea of your goals, where you want to go, by what means and how fast you want to reach these goals. And once you are clear about that, you have to have a proper balance sheet. Because there is a certain reality. You can say, to put it in practical terms so that it's easier to understand: "Let's build such-and-such number of schools, so that in five years' time we won't need a single additional school in Cuba. Let's build such-and-such number of houses, so that in five years' time we won't need a single additional house in Cuba. Let's build a merchant fleet, so that in five years' time we won't need a single additional ship in Cuba. Let's build such-and-such number of airplanes, so that in five years' time not a single foreign airplane will be needed in Cuba."

We can keep on making plans like that, but when we come to drawing up a balance sheet—that is, comparing all we want with what we can do—we see that this cannot be done. Because it is not materially possible to satisfy in five years' time all the needs of peoples who have hungered for centuries just for a crust of bread.

Then comes the stage of sitting down and balancing the plan out, taking out something here, taking out something there, trying to make sure that the plan gives the necessary emphasis to the points I indicated, the fourth point on the diagram—creation of enterprises that in turn create new means of production. But we must not neglect the other points, that is, the creation of means of production properly speaking, buying means of production abroad, even if it means holding back a bit the speed of the country's industrial development.

When you have all these things, it's still not a plan. You need at least two other very important ingredients. One is a guiding body. That is, in capitalist anarchy, a plan is impossible. Where two businessmen fight over a market and sacrifice everything to obtain this market, an internal market, there can be no plan. A plan by necessity must have unity of direction, a unity and firmness of leadership. In this country, this unity is provided by the Central Planning Board [Junta Central de Planificación—Juceplan] whose chairman is the prime minister himself and whose vice-chairman, I might add, is our deputy prime minister, Commander Raúl Castro. In other words, the highest political authorities in this country directly manage the plan, guide it, and give it the unity of command necessary for its fulfillment.

I remind you that we are engaged in the plan's preliminary tasks. The plan begins in 1962. We are gathering data, getting a clear idea of what we want and how we can get it in the framework of our bottom lines.

There is still one final factor without which an economic development plan is impossible in a socialist system, and that is understanding and support of the plan by the people. A plan is not a mechanical thing, the product of semimetaphysical, cold scientific labors in some office or laboratory and then transmitted downward. A plan is a living thing whose fundamental purpose is to find the country's idle reserves and put them to work in production. To do that you must galvanize the great factor of production—the people. The people must understand what we want, they must discuss our aims in each instance, present their counterviews; and once they have understood it and approved it, the plan can go forward. That is, the natural course is from the top down, but from there it returns from the bottom up.

In other words, the government leaders who are closely identified with their people consider what is best for the people and put that into numbers, more or less arbitrary though of course based on logic and judgment. These are then sent from the top down: for example, from the Central Planning Board to the Ministry of Industry, where the Ministry of Industry makes the corrections it deems appropriate since it is closer to certain aspects of real life than the other offices. From there it continues downward to the enterprises, which make other corrections. From the enterprises it goes to the factories, where other corrections are made. And from there it goes to the workers, who must have the final say on the plan.

That is, the carrying out of a plan is profoundly democratic and that is its essential foundation. In considering what is wanted in a development plan, no one in this country, or any country where there is social justice, proposes development for the sake of better personal incomes or personal successes. Development is to better the country so that each person individually will obtain a better income and a better life. If this is the case, everyone in the country has and must have an interest in the plan. Therefore, it must become known in detail; it must reach the masses, be discussed and studied, not mechanically approved.

I can give an example here of mechanical approval of a proposal. It may distress some compañeros, but if it is taken in a constructive spirit it will serve as a good example, since it is the antithesis of what a plan should be. I should note that this error was caused by enthusiasm, the euphoria of victory, the approach of May Day, and so on. But in terms of what a plan should be, let me say, it is the antithesis.

A few days ago, the compañeros of the Sugar Federation set the slogan "Six million tons of sugar by May Day." When I heard this report a few days ago—ten or twelve—I was astonished, because I knew how the sugar harvest was going. I called the general administrator of the Sugar Combines, who is the head of the Consolidated Sugar Industry, Compañero Menéndez, and he told me that it had been a workers' initiative, that he hadn't been consulted before it was proclaimed to the masses. It cannot be achieved. Today is April 30 and tomorrow is May 1. Four hundred thousand tons would have to be produced this very day to reach six million tons by tomorrow. It cannot be done.

Why was this error committed? Whatever the plan was,

it didn't reach the masses. Because when someone says six million tons and does the figures, he says: "Okay, we have five and a half million tons, we need half a million more; how much does each sugar mill have to produce?" Then he figures out how much each sugar mill has to produce. It comes in to the sugar mill, and the workers tell him: "We cannot make that amount. In the time between now and May 1 it is impossible to produce that amount."

The plan would have been automatically thrown out and that would have spared us this painful reality: that the revolution, the workers, who are the revolution's most important spokesmen, have said things that have not been carried out, that they have given the idea that there is a certain superficiality in the government's declarations. . . .

The plan, of course, is a general economic plan; it encompasses the country's entire economy. The industrialization of the country is part of the plan. Industrialization is based on hard facts.

Here too, as with planning, we might talk about different kinds of industrialization; and possibly there's a theory of industrialization. But we are a very practical people. Whatever I have learned, I have learned by doing. So I shall leave the detailed theoretical investigations to those wiser and with greater expertise. We can say precisely what industrialization means in our country and what its foundations are: the foundations of industrialization in a country with a socialized economy with a development plan. . . .

[*Utilizing a map, Guevara indicates the locations of the new enterprises to be built in Cuba.*]

This is the panorama of what the country is going to be, or what the country intends to be in the coming years. It is presented from an optimistic standpoint, always with the idea that the country will be able to develop peacefully and that the steady growth of the forces of peace will make an aggression more and more unlikely.

That's our hope, understandably enough, our deepest desire.

But we must realize that the reality is otherwise. In analyzing our problems, the problems of industrialization, one of the primary ones to consider is imperialist aggression. How far will that aggression go? I cannot say.

Mr. Kennedy's words are full of a profound conviction of special destiny, full of fascist bombast as well as arrogance and concentrated rage, because for the first time in the Americas he has not been able to easily accomplish his designs. We therefore don't know what the future attitude of the United States will be.

And that also has great importance from the standpoint of industrial construction, because we may have to add to the task of construction, that of reconstruction. What is certain is that victory will be ours. But we don't know how much destruction imperialist aggression will cause. . . .

In Cuba, technicians must be the most qualified in their field. In the United States technicians are a field set apart, situated between the great mass of the exploited and the small group of exploiters. They get more crumbs from the feast than do the workers, not only quantitatively, but qualitatively. . . .

That is why we are trying to create something entirely new. That is, a person who comes from the working class, from the peasantry, who is a product of the revolution. Those children who came out of the Sierra Maestra not knowing what an electric light was are today becoming trained operators of agricultural equipment in schools like the Camilo Cienfuegos School. They will be the foundation for the new, future technicians and they will feel totally at one with the people. They will not have the slightest feeling of inferiority or superiority toward anyone.

Our technicians have had their faults, but despite everything, despite the fact that technicians of the old type are not the ideal, we would have preferred such technicians to none at all. And in many cases we have had to resign ourselves to none at all. Because either there weren't any—in general there were far fewer than needed—or they left, and each day some are leaving. It is no secret to anybody that each day somebody takes the road of exile—either because he has been bought off, or, to be fair, because he simply can't take the "climate" in Cuba, an entirely new climate. I don't think it's as smooth a road as many imagine, but that is the reality.

So we have had a whole series of problems. These include a lack of technical knowledge and a low ideological consciousness on the part of technicians—who moreover are not that numerous. Thus economic progress has been hard and continues to be hard. We have had to resort to the training or semitraining en masse of compañeros with a poor fount of knowledge. We have had to teach people how to read and write and, after they have learned that, to give them responsibilities requiring considerable knowledge—at the very least reading, writing, and the techniques involved in their jobs. Everything must be created in this way. That is the great work of building the economy. That is the miracle a people can accomplish when they are filled with the sacred idea of production, with an entirely revitalized spirit, when they are put in the critical position of creating a new world under unfavorable conditions and at great speed—which is our situation. . . .

In addition, we have had the problem of the imperialist blockade of raw materials. All right, there are raw materials—I just pointed out that some of the raw materials we have are not meant for our machinery but we have had to adapt them. Why is this? Because there is an imperialist blockade. . . .

For example, they aren't selling us ammonia. And Cubanitro, which still hasn't finished its own ammonia plant—although it's in the process of doing so, can't suddenly get it imported from the Soviet Union. The imperialists know that ammonia is an industrial raw material in great demand. So Cubanitro has been paralyzed.

The same has happened to many other plants, and some function at half capacity. So in general our ambitious plans were not accomplished. We made our production plans on the assumption that we would have all the necessary raw materials and spare parts. We set out enthusiastically to achieve this plan—a plan that was not announced because it was a preliminary plan to prepare for the actual development plan beginning in 1962.

We suffered from a defect like the one I pointed out a little while ago to the leading compañeros and workers in the sugar sector. We did not go to the masses. We made a laboratory-type plan. We calculated installed capacity. We calculated production. We saw what could be increased. And that was our work plan, which I have made public today. Its goals were not announced precisely because they were still being worked out. But they had this defect. We see it clearly today: The masses did not participate in drawing up the plan. And a plan in which the masses do not participate is a plan in serious danger of failure. . . .

We realized the plan by only 25 percent. That is, we achieved one-fourth of the plan. However, if we take 1960 as 100, that plan, which was one-fourth realized, came to 175. A plan that was three-fourths a failure nevertheless brought about a 75 percent increase in one year, which is a fabulous sum. What does this teach us? One thing basically: the extraordinary amount of idle installed capacity that exists in Cuba. . . .

We failed in our attempt to put all our installed capacity to work because we did not have sufficient raw materials and because we did not go sufficiently to the masses to discuss our plans—even these limited plans. All this experience can be put to use in coming up with the great four-year plan. . . .

We have talked about almost all the problems of industrialization. Now I want to emphasize relations with the workers.

We have already seen the urgent need for relations with the masses. But, of course, this is not a fault on our side alone. It is a fault on both sides. The working class is still not fully conscious of its strength, its potential, its duties, and its rights. . . .

We are in an epoch in which the revolution has proclaimed itself socialist, and socialism is not a word but is the product of economic deeds and deeds of consciousness. That is why we must do a great deal more work on this aspect.

For example, we have a creation of the revolution—a few days ago I was reading a little news sheet we have here. It's hardly worth mentioning, but it's a Trotskyist newspaper whose name I'm not sure of. [Voice in background tells him it is *Voz Proletaria.*] *Voz Proletaria.* It criticized the Technical Advisory Committees from a Trotskyist point of view. It said that the Technical Advisory Committees were created by the timorous petty bourgeoisie in the government in order to give something to the masses, who are demanding the right to run the factories—without in reality giving them anything.

Now from the theoretical standpoint, that is an absurdity and from the practical standpoint it is a slander, or else a gross mistake.* The trouble in fact with the Technical

* The Cuban group criticized by Guevara could more accurately be called Posadists; its members were all followers of Juan Posadas, an Argentine, who early in 1962 split the Cuban group and several other Latin American groups away from the Fourth International, the world Trotskyist organization. The split-off Posadist movement dubbed itself the Fourth International and became increasingly hostile to the Castro government. The Posadists were denounced as sectarian and ultraleft by the authentic Fourth International, which was and remains an ardent defender of Cuba's revolutionary regime.

Advisory Committees is that they were not created by the pressure of the masses: They were bureaucratically created from above to give the masses a vehicle they had not asked for, and that is the fault of the masses. We, the "timorous petty bourgeoisie," went looking for a channel that would enable us to listen to the masses' voice. And we created the Technical Advisory Committees, for better or worse, with the imperfections they very likely have, because they were our idea, our creation. That is, they were the creation of people who lack experience in these problems. What was not present at all, and I want to stress this, was pressure from the masses. There must be pressure from the masses in a whole series of things. Because the masses must take an interest in finding out what a plan is, what industrialization is, what each factory must do, what their own obligation is, and how this obligation can be increased or decreased, and what the interests of the working class are in every factory. All these are problems that must stir the masses.

The masses must be constantly abreast of what is happening in their work centers and be able to relate it to the overall life of the nation.

We intend to continue discussions in order to increase the effectiveness of the Technical Advisory Committees, which today has added importance because of the fact that they are now involved in the Spare Parts Committees, also created from above by the revolution. We want to establish ties—not ties because ties are very narrow. We want to establish instruments of expression that will enable the masses to make themselves heard automatically at the top. Because one thing is certain: somebody up in a ministry, closed in, with air conditioning and all those things, cannot hear the pulse of the workers. That is why we are looking for instruments of expression.

We are trying in every way possible to overcome this situation, to make the working class feel a deep involvement in their revolution. And for this we have two very important plans—one will be announced within a few days to the public. We have the national emulation plan and the workers' educational plan.

What do these consist of? I'll jump the gun. The national emulation plan is divided into two stages. Its second stage, which has previously been announced, will be a technical plan that will involve work norms, and these norms will have rewards along with them. In all, there will be a perfect synchronization between production, productivity, and reward. This reward is fundamentally a moral incentive. There will also be a material incentive.

The first stage of the emulation plan, which is the important one, is the organizational stage. What must workers' emulation center around today? Keeping their factories clean; keeping their machines in perfect condition; giving thought to replacement parts and seeing how they can be made; seeing that raw materials are secured; replacing raw materials when not imported; guarding their work centers, not just their machines but their work centers, as collective organs of production, from any attempts at sabotage; joining the revolutionary organizations that defend the revolution; raising their technical level—raising their technical level above all—contributing with their work, their brains, and their head to the country's production.

All this will be laid out in a plan, as I say, in two stages. The first stage is the organization of the emulation plan. The second is emulation, properly speaking, technically worked out.

The education plan includes from the lowest levels—we are not going to divide this up into levels, that is also a bad habit, petty bourgeois, as the Trotskyist compañeros say—from the lowest to the highest technical capabilities.

For example, we are starting with the technical minimum. What is the technical minimum? The capability an individual needs to operate the machines on his job. After that, a series of primary schools will be established; after that, high schools, then universities, which will bring the worker along in an uninterrupted chain, from an illiterate worker who reaches the technical minimum to a highly qualified engineer, or to the president of the republic or whatever, through a continuous chain in which work and study together train the workers technically and educate them in every sense.

That is the great task not only of the Ministry of Industry; the Ministry of Industry has what we could call the initial part in the plan. That is, it must seek the worker with an inquiring mind and give him initial instruction, establish schools of elementary administration. After this it is the turn of the Ministry of Education—or he should go to the Council of Ministers—or to some other higher body such as the Central Planning Board for specific kinds of advanced study.

All this looks nice on paper. But like everything else, many of these things don't turn out in practice as well as they are described on paper. What is fundamental in all this, however, is that this work could not be done without two things: One is the determination of the country itself, all of it. The other is the help of the socialist countries. Both are completely bound together and complementary, since naturally the socialist countries offer their aid because they see that our country is eager to improve, to liberate itself. And when our country feels that it has support from the socialist countries, it feels more secure, shows greater firmness, a greater urge to accomplish things; and more help comes from the socialist countries. But these are two highly interconnected things.

A struggle of blows and counterblows brought the Cuban people very rapidly from the revolution of high ideals—which for a few months was no danger to imperialism—to our present extremely profound socialist revolution, which owns the means of production and plans the economy in its totality. This is the road our country has traveled. We have been so directly involved that we often can neither measure nor gauge the stages. . . .

Of course, now is not the time to define socialism. As far as we are concerned, the job and the obligation of the Ministry of Industry is to know that socialism is characterized by the people owning the means of production, which are at the service of the people. Naturally, we will have to talk a lot about these questions related to the new historical stage we are living through. We will have to explain very clearly that, besides the purely economic side, there is a side having to do with consciousness, which is of the utmost importance.

I hope that personally—I think the prime minister will close this lecture series—that he, or if not he then some other compañero, will give a clear explanation of all these questions. But it is important to stress that unless the people are clearly conscious of their rights and duties in this new stage, we cannot truly attain, cannot really work in the kind of socialist society we aspire to—a socialist society that is absolutely democratic, that is democratic by definition, because it bases itself on the needs and aspirations of the people and where the people play a determining role in all decisions. . . .

At Punta del Este

The Inter-American Economic and Social Conference, sponsored by the Organization of American States, was held at Punta del Este, Uruguay, during August 1961. There the Kennedy administration sought to repair U.S. prestige damaged by the failure of the Bay of Pigs invasion and to stem the spread of revolution to the rest of Latin America. In the hope of accomplishing these aims, the U.S. State Department was presenting its proposed Alliance for Progress to the conference for official ratification. Though U.S. diplomacy was striving to ostracize Cuba, it would be another six months before it would be able to bring about that country's expulsion from the OAS. Consequently, C. Douglas Dillon, the U.S. representative at Punta del Este, had to suffer the presence of a Cuban delegation headed by Che Guevara. The selections below are from Guevara's speech delievered on August 8, 1961.

I must say that Cuba's interpretation is that this is a political conference. Cuba does not agree that economics can be separated from politics, and understands that they always go

Oceanside Public Library

Checked Out Items 9/11/2017 15:27
XXXXXXXXXX4938

Item Title	Due Date
31232009245038	10/2/2017 23:59
! Che Guevara speaks	
31232006681912	10/2/2017 23:59
Samurai warfare	

760-435-5600
www.oceansidepubliclibrary.org

together. That is why you cannot have technicians who speak of techniques when the destinies of a people are at stake. And I am also going to explain why this conference is political. It is political because all economic conferences are political. But it is also political because it was conceived against Cuba, and because it has been conceived to counter the example that Cuba represents throughout Latin America.

And if there is any doubt about that, on the tenth, in Fort Amador in the [Panama] Canal Zone, General Decker, while instructing a group of Latin American military men in the art of repressing the people, spoke of the technical conference in Montevideo and said that it had to be backed.

But that's nothing. In the inaugural message on August 5, 1961, President Kennedy asserted: "Those of you at this conference are present at an historic moment in the life of this Hemisphere. For this is far more than an economic discussion, or a technical conference on development. In a very real sense it is a demonstration of the capacity of free nations to meet the human and material problems of the modern world."

I could continue with the quotation of the prime minister of Peru, where he also refers to political themes. But in order not to tire the distinguished delegates, for I can foresee that my presentation will be a bit long, I will refer to some statements made by the "technicians"—a term we place within quotes—on point 5 of the draft text.

At the end of page 11, it is stated as a definitive conclusion: "To establish, on a hemispheric and national level, regular consultative procedures with the trade union advisory committees, so that they may play an influential role in the political formulation of programs that might be approved in the special session."

And to drive home my point, so that there may not remain any doubt as to my right to speak of political matters—which is what I plan to do in the name of the Cuban government—here is a quotation from page 7 of that same report on point 5 in question:

"Delay in accepting the responsibility of the democratic information media to defend the essential values of our civilization, without any weakening or commitments of a material sort, would signify irreparable damage to democratic society and the imminent danger of the disappearance of the freedoms enjoyed today, as has occurred in Cuba . . ."—Cuba is spelled out—". . . where today all newspapers, radio, television, and movies are controlled by the absolute power of the government."

In other words, distinguished delegates, in the report we are to discuss, Cuba is put on trial from a political point of view. Very well then, Cuba will state its truths from a political point of view, and from an economic point of view, as well. . . .

All right, gentlemen technicians, fellow delegates, the time has come to address the economic section of the text. Point 1 is very broad. Prepared by very brainy technicians, it aims at planning the social and economic development of Latin America.

I'm going to refer to some of the statements of the gentlemen technicians in order to refute them from the technical point of view, and then present the Cuban delegation's viewpoint on what development planning is.

The first incongruity that we observe in this work is expressed in this passage:

"Sometimes the idea is expressed that an increase in the level and in the diversity of economic activity necessarily results in the improvement of sanitary conditions. Nevertheless, the group is of the opinion that the improvement of sanitary conditions is not only desirable per se, but that it constitutes an indispensable prerequisite to economic growth, and that it should therefore form an essential part of the programs for the development of the region."

On the other hand, this is also reflected in the structure of the loans granted by the Inter-American Development Bank, for in the analysis that we made of the $120 million loaned in the first period, $40 million, in other words one-third, corresponds directly to loans of this type; for housing, for aqueducts, for sewers.

It's a bit like . . . I don't know, but I would almost classify it as a colonial condition. I get the impression that they are thinking of making the latrine the fundamental thing. That would improve the social conditions of the poor Indian, of the poor black, of the poor person who lives under subhuman conditions. "Let's make latrines for them and after we've made latrines for them, and after their education has taught them how to keep them clean, then they can enjoy the benefits of production." Because it should be noted, distinguished delegates, that the topic of industrialization does not figure in the analysis of the distinguished technicians. Planning for the gentlemen technicians is the planning of latrines. As for the rest, who knows how it will be done!

If the president will allow me, I will express my deepest regrets in the name of the Cuban delegation for the loss of the services of such an efficient technician as the one who directed this first group, Dr. Felipe Pazos. With his intelligence and capacity for work, and with our revolutionary activity, within two years Cuba could have become the paradise of the latrine, even if we did not have a single one of the 250 factories that we are beginning to build, even if we had not carried out the agrarian reform.

I ask myself, distinguished delegates, if they aren't trying to make fun of us—not of Cuba, because Cuba is not included, since the Alliance for Progress is not for Cuba but against her, and since it is not established to give one cent to Cuba—but if they aren't trying to make fun of all the rest of the delegates.

Don't you get the impression, just a little bit, that your

leg is being pulled? You are given dollars to build highways, you are given dollars to build roads, you are given dollars to dig sewers. Gentlemen, what do you build roads with, what do you dig the sewers with, what do you build houses with? You don't have to be a genius for that. Why don't they give dollars for equipment, dollars for machinery, dollars so that our underdeveloped countries, all of them, can become industrial-agricultural countries, at one and the same time? Really, it's sad.

On page 10, in the part about the planning of development under point 6, it is made evident who the real author of this plan is. Point 6 says: "To establish more solid bases for the granting and utilization of external financial aid, especially to provide effective criteria to evaluate individual projects."

We are not going to establish the most solid foundations for granting and utilization, because *we* are not the ones granting; you here are the ones who are receiving, not granting. We, Cuba, are watching, and it is the United States that is making the grants. This point 6, then, is drafted directly by the United States. It is the recommendation of the United States, and this is the spirit of the whole abortive scheme called point 1.

But I want to impress upon you one thing. We have spoken a good deal about politics. We have denounced what is a political plot here. We have emphasized in conversations with the distinguished delegates Cuba's right to express these opinions, because Cuba is directly attacked in point 5. Nevertheless, Cuba does not come here to sabotage the meeting, as some of the newspapers or many of the mouthpieces of the foreign information agencies are claiming.

Cuba comes to condemn what is worthy of condemnation from the point of view of principles. But Cuba also comes to work harmoniously, if possible, in order to straighten out this thing that has been born so twisted, and Cuba is ready to collaborate with all the distinguished delegates to set it right and make it into a beautiful project.

The honorable Mr. Douglas Dillon in his speech cited financing; that is important. We must speak of financing if we are all to get together and speak of development, and we have all assembled here to talk with the one country that has the capital for financing.

Mr. Dillon says: "Looking at the years to come and at the sources of external financing—international entities such as Europe and Japan as much as the United States; new private investments and investments of public funds—if Latin America takes as a precondition the necessary internal measures, it can logically expect that its efforts . . ." (He doesn't even say, "if it takes these measures, this will happen," but only "it can logically expect"!)" . . . will be matched by an influx of capital on the order of at least $20 billion in the next ten years, with the majority of these funds coming from official sources."

Is this how much there is? No, only $500 million are approved; this is what is being talked about. This must be emphasized, because it is the nub of the question. What does it mean? And I assure you that I'm not asking this for us, but for the good of all. What does it mean "if Latin America takes the necessary internal measures"? And what does "it can logically expect" mean?

I think that later in the work of the committees or at a time that the representative of the United States deems opportune, this detail should be cleared up a little, because $20 billion is an interesting sum. It is no less than two-thirds of the figure that our prime minister announced as necessary for the development of the Americas; push it a little more and we arrive at $30 billion. [*Laughter*] But that $30 billion has to arrive in jingling cash, dollar by dollar, into the national coffers of each one of the countries of the Americas, with the exception of this poor Cinderella who probably will receive nothing. [*Laughter*]

That's where we can help, not in a plan of blackmail, such as is foreseen, because it is said: "Cuba is the goose that lays the golden egg. Cuba exists, and while there is a Cuba, the United States will continue to give." No, we don't come here for that reason. We come to work, to try and struggle on the level of principles and ideas, for the development of our peoples. Because all or nearly all of the distinguished representatives have said it: if the Alliance for Progress fails, nothing can hold back the wave of popular movements—I say this in my own words, but that's what was meant. Nothing can hold back the wave of popular movements if the Alliance for Progress fails. And we are interested in it not failing, if and insofar as it means a real improvement for Latin America in the standard of living of all its 200 million inhabitants. I can make this statement honestly and with all sincerity.

We have diagnosed and foreseen the social revolution in the Americas, the real one, because events are unfolding in a different way, because there is an attempt to hold the people back with bayonets, and when the people realize that they can take the bayonets and turn them against the ones who brandish them, then those who brandish them are lost. But if the road that the people want to take is one of logical and harmonious development, through long-term loans with low interest, as Mr. Dillon said, with fifty years to pay, we also are in agreement.

The only thing is, distinguished delegates, that we all have to work together here to make that figure concrete, and to make sure that the Congress of the United States approves it. Because don't forget that we are faced with a presidential and parliamentary regime, not a "dictatorship" like Cuba, where a representative of Cuba stands up, speaks in the name of his government, and takes responsibility for his actions. What is said here also has to be ratified over there, and the experience of all the distinguished delegates is that many times the promises made here were not approved there. [*Applause*] . . .

And to all of you, distinguished delegates, the Cuban delegation says with all frankness: we wish, on our conditions, to be within the Latin American family. We want to live with Latin America. We want to see you grow, if possible, at the same rate that we are growing, but we don't oppose your growing at another rate. What we do demand is the guarantee of nonaggression for our borders.

We cannot stop exporting our example, as the United States wants, because an example is something intangible that crosses borders. What we do guarantee is that we will not export revolution. We guarantee that not one rifle will be moved from Cuba, that not one weapon will be moved from Cuba for fighting in any other country in Latin America.

What we cannot guarantee is that the idea of Cuba will not take root in some other country of Latin America, and what we do guarantee this conference is that if urgent measures of social prevention are not taken, the example of Cuba will take root in the people. And then that statement that once gave people a lot to think about, which Fidel made one July 26 and which was interpreted as an aggression, will again be true. Fidel said that if the social conditions continued as they have been until now, "the Andes would become the Sierra Maestra of Latin America."

Distinguished delegates, we call for an Alliance for Progress, an alliance for our progress, a peaceful alliance for the progress of all. We are not opposed to being left out in the distribution of loans, but we are opposed to being left out in participating in the cultural and spiritual life of our Latin American people, to whom we belong.

What we will never allow is a restriction on our freedom to trade and have relations with all the peoples of the world. And we will defend ourselves with all our strength against any attempt at foreign aggression, be it from an imperial power or be it from some Latin American body that concurs in the desire of some to see us wiped out.

To conclude, Mr. President, distinguished delegates, I want to tell you that some time ago we had a meeting of the general staff of the Revolutionary Armed Forces in my country, a general staff to which I belong. An aggression against Cuba was being discussed, which we knew would come, but we did not know when or where. We thought it would be very big; in fact it was going to be very big. This happened prior to the famous warning of the premier of the Soviet Union, Nikita Khrushchev, that their rockets could fly beyond the Soviet borders. We had not asked for that aid and we did not know about that readiness to aid us. Therefore, we met knowing that the invasion was coming, in order to face our final destiny as revolutionaries.

We knew that if the United States invaded Cuba, there would be a massive slaughter, but that in the end we would be defeated and expelled from every inhabited place in the country. We then proposed, the members of the general staff, that Fidel Castro retire to a secure place in the mountains and that one of us take charge of the defense of Havana. Our prime minister and leader answered at that time—with words that exalt him, as do all his acts—that if the United States invaded Cuba and Havana was defended as it should be defended, hundreds of thousands of men, women, and children would die before the drive of the Yankees' weapons, and that the leader of a people in revolution could not be asked to take shelter in the mountains; that his place was there, where the cherished dead were to be found, and that there, with them, he would fulfill his historic mission.

That invasion did not take place, but we maintain that spirit, distinguished delegates. For that reason I can predict that the Cuban revolution is invincible, because it has a people and because it has a leader like the one leading Cuba.

That is all, distinguished delegates.

Cuba and the Kennedy Plan

The following excerpts are from Guevara's balance sheet of the Punta del Este Conference. It was originally published in English in *World Marxist Review* of February 1962.

Unable to strangle the revolution, the United States set out to isolate Cuba in order to make short shrift of it later. The Inter-American Economic and Social Conference, held in Punta del Este, Uruguay, in August 1961, was the preparation for this isolation. It aimed to demonstrate clearly that Cuba need not be reckoned with, that it had come only to boycott the conference and, acting "on orders from Moscow," to prevent the North Americans from granting "generous" loans to the Latin American countries. . . .

The conference opened with plenary meetings that dealt with the usual things one says at this type of assembly. In our opinion only four of the speeches were really worthy of attention for those who closely follow Latin American events.

One of them was delivered by the Bolivian delegate, who criticized the imperialist system insofar as permitted by Bolivia's dependence on the United States. He advanced a number of interesting ideas and declared that his government intended in the next few years to increase per capita income by 5 percent annually.

The second speech was by the delegate of Ecuador, who roundly criticized U.S. policy in Latin America for its past attitude, as well as criticizing the U.S. delegation at present.

The third noteworthy speech was that of [U.S. delegation head] Dillon, who was assigned to announce what was going to be done. His speech was very vague, without a single paragraph of substance.

"If we look forward and examine the external sources of capital—the international credit institutions, European countries, Japan, and the U.S.A., and take into account the likelihood of private and public investments—and if Latin America takes the necessary internal measures, these countries can expect an influx of capital of at least $20 billion in the next ten years. Most of these investments will come from government sources."

As one can see, there's the condition expressed in the sentence, "if Latin America takes the necessary internal measures." The characteristics of this condition were not clearly explained, so its interpretation rests with the Yankee whim.

There were also a few mentions of agrarian reform (à la Washington) and the aim was expressed of exploring the possibility of concluding agreements on purchasing products such as coffee and tin. The rest was empty verbiage.

Dillon's speech expressed, to a certain extent, a new tendency in U.S. policy, one of modifying the system by which the Latin American peoples are exploited, and of shifting its relations away from feudalist forces and toward different sections of the parasitic bourgeoisie. The aim is to lessen internal discontent in each Latin American country by making minor concessions to the people and to sacrifice the most backward sections of society in the interests of the national bourgeoisie, on condition that these countries surrender their interests completely and renounce their own development. This tendency found expression in the so-called Kennedy Plan, which the president himself has given the pompous title of "Alliance for Progress." It was presented as the latest word in U.S. policy, although in reality it does not represent any change whatsoever in the traditional imperialist essence of this policy.

It cannot be said, however, that this tendency has prevailed completely in U.S. Latin American policy. The U.S. monopolies consider the old method of exploitation the most reliable one. They know it well and don't find it easy to try "innovations" that pursue the same ends but seek to dress them up in sheep's clothing.

It is important to point this out, because the Punta del Este conference has given rise to greater hopes than previous gatherings, and we might believe that this is something new, or the result of a new U.S. policy. . . .

After analyzing the four key items on the agenda, Cuba announced it would explain in more detail why it considered that the present Inter-American Economic and Social Conference was political in character and why its ultimate objective was isolating Cuba. We read out parts of two secret U.S. documents, which we had received through our friends and which now are known to the whole world. One of these documents, of a working character, was primarily meant for internal use. In it was expressed the plans of the imperialist forces and their scorn for our governments and for the "natives."

The second document was an official State Department analysis of the situation on the continent after the Playa Girón defeat. It is objective enough, as the imperialists sometimes know how to do when they draft secret documents, and it reflects some truths basic to an understanding of the subsequent course of events. In the official State Department document, it says that Cuba could not be an aggressor. It even brazenly admits that Cuba's military preparations were purely defensive in anticipation of another invasion; that these present no danger to other countries. What is dangerous is Cuba's example, Castro's ability to demonstrate the superiority of his regime. . . .

The document clearly reveals the details of imperialist machinations: At present the tactical objective is complete isolation of Cuba because what matters is the Cuban example; the tactical obstacles to the realization of this objective are Brazil and Mexico. . . .

In this way we finally came to the end of the initial plenary and there began the tedious and unproductive discussions in the commissions. . . .

In each of the commissions Cuba submitted deep-going proposals that not only hit at the U.S. position, but also at times created dangerous restlessness among the delegates. Fear of Cuba was total. At times, one or another delegation would, in veiled fashion, appropriate a proposal originally submitted by Cuba, without naming us. Then some other country would refer to the position put forward by the delegate of such and such a country, forgetting that Cuba was the original proponent. This served a purpose, naturally, because now the proposal could be introduced in full or in part, as long as Cuba wasn't the one that presented it. . . .

In each of the commissions we had to fight every inch of the way, but, curiously enough, rarely on ideological issues. We were forced to fight against the rules of procedure, against arbitrary interpretation of these rules, against the frequent tendency to "forget" to include certain paragraphs in the resolutions; to fight to have representatives of our delegation in the working commissions and to ensure that these commissions did not forget to invite them to their sittings.

In short, we had to talk and talk endlessly, unopposed by any competitors. They merely listened and voted. . . .

At the final plenary session the Cuban delegation abstained from voting on all of the documents and took the floor to explain the reasons for this. We made it clear that Cuba could not subscribe to the "monetary policy" or the principle of free enterprise proclaimed in these documents. We pointed out that the final document did not attack the imperialist monopolies that were the cause of the evils we faced, nor did it condemn the aggression against us. Moreover, there was no answer to the question put by our delegation as to whether Cuba could or could not take part [in the "Alliance for Progress"]. Silence was the response, which we took as a negative reply to the question. For this reason the Cuban delegation stated that it could not participate in an alliance that offered nothing to our people. . . .

How does Cuba evaluate the results of this conference, and what can Latin America expect? While Cuba should not feel it was a complete failure, we can't in any way say that it was a great victory for the Latin American peoples.

Imperialism had to demonstrate Cuba's incapacity to live in peace with the rest of Latin America in the framework of the OAS, and its refusal to exchange opinions with the other countries. They did not achieve this, so from this point of view they lost the battle. Analyzing the secret documents read out by our delegation, it's clear that imperialism did not expect to convince Brazil to change its stance on Cuba.

Even though there were new expressions of insubordination, the United States was able to manage the situation in such a way that the final declaration made it appear that they had conceded a great gift to us Latin Americans, even though the rules governing this gift are full of clauses that make it worthless. In other words, without committing itself officially to anything, the United States appears as the supplier of $20 billion over the next ten years. It has been able to maintain its position in Latin America more or less secure, at the governmental level to be sure, since the people continually grow in political consciousness—that is, consciousness of the need to get rid of imperialism. The Cuban proposals were defeated in most cases by a vote of 20 against 1.

What conclusions can we draw for the future from this conference? We should state that even in the remote event of the $20 billion promise being kept, the "Alliance for Progress" would use this amount to finance a number of imperialist enterprises so they can develop their activities throughout Latin America, whether acting directly as foreign enterprises or as joint ventures, in this way continuing to take in fabulous profits.

In all probability the prices of raw materials of which the United States is the principal buyer will also keep falling. This prediction can be safely made since the supply on the world market of raw materials produced in Latin America (coffee, cotton, tin, etc.) exceeds the demand. Plus the tendency is to develop new areas (for instance, coffee plantations in Africa).

The U.S. monopolies' profits signify an export of dollars abroad. On top of this, the lowering of the prices of raw materials signifies fewer dollars coming in. Therefore there will be a greater or lesser deterioration in the balance of payments for nearly all Latin American countries. Moreover, the tendency is for the discrepancy between investments and exports of profits to grow.

This translates into lack of development. And every year that passes, there will be higher unemployment and more competition for markets. This competition will become very violent, especially at times of crisis.

From here on in, whenever a country needs help from international finance organizations for its shattered economy, the International Monetary Fund will step in, give its "wise and considered" opinion, and tighten even more its control over the economy of the country. Domestic credits will be curtailed, and the economy will be brought in line with the interests of the monopolies. This will happen sooner or later in every country of Latin America.

There is only one alternative: To save their countries from disaster, the national bourgeoisie must radically change their trade policies. But in doing so, they must also reshape diplomatic efforts accordingly. Moreover, national capitalism would have to be developed to the maximum where this is possible, to try to ameliorate the current conditions in society, at least for a time.

But even if this is done, there is still another factor to be reckoned with, a factor whose importance was dramatically highlighted in Brazil after the Punta del Este conference. This factor is the army in each country of Latin America.

As an instrument of the old feudal oligarchies or the importing bourgeoisie, the army actively seeks to prevent new sections of the national industrial bourgeoisie from taking power and pursuing their own policy, repressing them immediately. In nearly all Latin American countries the armed forces are hostile to the most elementary manifestations of independence, since their command is closely linked with the darkest forces of reaction in Latin America and the interests of the U.S. monopolists.

One thing is clear: To implement a progressive policy in international relations and foreign trade, the national bourgeoisies must institute internal measures to free their policy and raise, at least slightly, the people's standard of living. But they need something more. At the very least, they need the army's neutrality.

What is the other road for the semicolonial governments? Simply put, to follow the dictates of the IMF, establish tighter and tighter controls that strangle credit, increase unemployment, and put the country in a situation of stagnation and retreat . . . and confront popular rage.

We can see two possible ways out. One is the road of several countries that are dependent on the United States but dependent also on certain rules of bourgeois institutionalism. So through free elections, the government can be delivered into the hands of its successors. Naturally the successor will have spoken during the election campaign as President [Jânio] Quadros did—he will have made promises and will try to carry them out.

But what will happen? Once again we will face the dilemma: either suppress the oppressor army or it will not be possible to implement an independent policy in Latin America. But to change the army, unfortunately as we see it, it will be necessary to fight, since they have the arms. It represents classes that are historically doomed, but who do not want to abandon their prerogatives without a struggle.

The other possibility is that a new military dictatorship might be set up, or an existing dictatorship consolidated in defiance of the people's wishes, intensify the exploitation of man by man, and increase the plunder of the national bourgeoisie and the lower classes of the population by the foreign monopolies. And to repress and repress to the ultimate degree.

The working people of each Latin American country subjected to this system will day by day increase their desire to free themselves from oppression. From afar, they will see the example of Cuba as well as other examples, more distant perhaps, even more compelling—the great examples of the socialist countries and especially of the Soviet Union, which took the first step toward the liberation of mankind. Quietly and full of wrath, the working people will go forward until some day, some place, the spark will ignite and a new revolutionary flame will be lit in the Americas. Forging ahead fatefully with the rapid steps of history during this convulsive moment for humanity, that day is approaching for all Latin America.

Cadres for the new party

The French word *cadre* meaning framework, especially in the sense of the skeletal force of noncomissioned officers of a regiment, which needs only to be fleshed out with enough recruits to become a fully functioning unit, has made its way into the military vocabulary of most countries and into the political parlance of revolutionary movements throughout the world.

Unlike previous revolutions of this century, the Cuban revolution had to build its party after coming to power. Here, Guevara discusses the problems of selecting the cadre, i.e., that core of trained, active, and responsible members that will educate the new recruits and that will embody the party's stability and continuity. The excerpts are from Guevara's article, "Cadres: Backbone of the Revolution," in the September 1962 issue of *Cuba Socialista.*

It is not necessary to dwell on the characteristics of our revolution, on the original way, with strokes of spontaneity, that the transition took place from a revolution of national liberation to a socialist revolution. Nor on the accumulation of rapidly passing stages in the course of its development, led by the same people who participated in the initial epic of the attack on the Moncada garrison, proceeding through the *Granma* landing, and culminating in the declaration of the socialist character of the Cuban revolution. New sympathizers, cadres, and organizations joined the weak organizational structure of the early movement, until it became the flood of people that today characterizes our revolution.

When it became clear that a new social class had definitively taken command in Cuba, we also saw the great limitations that would be faced in the exercise of state power because of the conditions in which we found the state. There were no cadres to carry out the enormous number of jobs that had to be filled in the state apparatus, in the political organization, and on the entire economic front.

Immediately after the seizure of power, bureaucratic posts were filled simply by "pointing a finger." There were no major problems—there were none because the old structure had not yet been shattered. The apparatus functioned at the slow and weary pace of something old and almost lifeless. But it had an organization and within it sufficient coordination to maintain itself through inertia, disdaining the political changes that were taking place as a prelude to the change in the economic structure.

The July 26 Movement, deeply wounded by the internal struggles between its right and left wings, could not devote itself to tasks of construction. And the Popular Socialist Party, because it had endured fierce attacks and illegality for years, had not been able to develop intermediate cadres to handle the newly arising responsibilities.

When the first state interventions in the economy took place, the task of finding cadres was not very complicated, and it was possible to choose from among many people who had some minimum basis for exercising positions of leadership.

But with the acceleration of the process beginning with the nationalization of the U.S. enterprises and later of the large Cuban enterprises, a real hunger for administrative technicians came about. On the other hand, an urgent need was felt for production technicians because of the exodus of many who were attracted by better positions offered by the imperialist companies in other parts of Latin America or in the United States itself. While engaged in these organizational tasks, the political apparatus had to make intense efforts to provide ideological attention to the masses who had joined the revolution eager to learn.

We all performed our roles as well as we could, but not without problems and embarrassments. Many errors were committed in administrative areas on the central executive level. Enormous mistakes were made by the new administrators of enterprises, who had overwhelming responsibilities in their hands. We also committed big and costly errors in the political apparatus, which little by little degenerated into a pleasant and peaceful bureaucracy, seen almost as a springboard for promotions and for bureaucratic posts of greater or lesser importance, totally separated from the masses.

The main cause of our errors was our lack of a sense of reality at a given moment. But the tool that we lacked, which blunted our ability to see and was turning the party into a bureaucratic organization, endangering administration and production, was the lack of developed cadres at the intermediate level. It became evident that the development of cadres was synonymous with the policy of going to the masses. The watchword was to once again establish contact with the masses, a contact that had been closely maintained by the revolution in its earliest days. But this had to be established through some type of mechanism that would afford the most beneficial results, both in feeling the pulse of the masses and in the transmission of political leadership, which in many cases was only being given through the personal intervention of Prime Minister Fidel Castro or some other leaders of the revolution.

At this point, we can pose the question: What is a cadre? We should state that a cadre is an individual who has achieved sufficient political development to be able to interpret the larger directives emanating from the central authority, make them his own, and convey them as an orientation to the masses; a person who at the same time also perceives the signs manifested by the masses of their own desires and their innermost motivations.

A cadre is someone of ideological and administrative discipline, who knows and practices democratic centralism and who knows how to evaluate the contradictions in our current methods in order to make the best of them. In the field of production, he knows how to practice the principle of collective discussion and individual decision making and responsibility. He is an individual of proven loyalty, whose physical and moral courage has developed in step with his ideological development, in such a way that he is always willing to face any debate and to give even his life for the good of the revolution. He is, in addition, an individual who can think for himself, which enables him to make the necessary decisions and to exercise creative initiative in a way that does not conflict with discipline.

The cadre, therefore, is a creator, a leader of high standing, a technician with a good political level, who by reasoning dialectically can advance his sector of production, or develop the masses from his position of political leadership.

This exemplary human being, apparently cloaked in difficult-to-achieve virtues, is nonetheless present in the people of Cuba, and we encounter him daily. The essential thing is to take advantage of all the opportunities that exist to develop him to the maximum, to educate him, to draw from each individual the greatest benefit and convert it into the greatest value for the nation.

The development of a cadre is achieved through performing everyday tasks. But the tasks must be undertaken systematically, in special schools where competent teachers—examples in their own right for the students—will encourage the most rapid ideological advancement.

In a system that is beginning to build socialism, cadres must clearly be highly developed politically. But when we consider political development we must take into account not only knowledge of Marxist theory. We must also demand responsibility of the individual for his actions, a discipline that restrains any passing weaknesses and that is not at odds with a big dose of initiative. And we must demand constant preoccupation with all the revolution's problems. In order to develop a cadre, we must begin by establishing the principle of selection among the masses. It is there that we find the individuals who are developing, tested by sacrifice or just beginning to show their concerns, and assign them to special schools; or when these are not available, give them greater responsibility so that they are tested in practical work.

In this way, we have been finding a multitude of new cadres who have developed in recent years. But their development has not been an even one, since the young compañeros have had to face the reality of revolutionary creation without an adequate party leadership. Some have succeeded fully, but there were others who could not completely make it and were left midway, or were simply lost in the bureaucratic labyrinth, or in the temptations that power brings.

To assure the triumph and the total consolidation of the revolution, we have to develop different types of cadres. We need the political cadre who will be the foundation of our mass organizations, and who will lead the masses through the action of the United Party of the Socialist Revolution. (We are already beginning to establish this foundation with the national and provincial Schools of Revolutionary Instruction and with studies and study groups at all levels.) We also need military cadres. To achieve that, we can utilize the selection the war made among our young combatants, since there are still many living who are without great theoretical knowledge but who were tested under fire. They were tested under the most difficult conditions of the struggle, with a fully proven loyalty to the revolutionary regime with whose birth and development they have been so intimately connected since the first guerrilla battles of the Sierra. We should also develop economic cadres who will dedicate themselves specifically to the difficult tasks of planning and the tasks of the organization of the socialist state in these moments of creation.

It is necessary to work with the professionals, urging the youth to follow one of the more important technical careers in an effort to give science the energy of ideological enthusiasm that will guarantee accelerated development. And it is imperative to create an administrative team that will know how to take advantage of and adapt the special technical knowledge of others and guide the enterprises and other organizations of the state to bring them into step with the powerful rhythm of the revolution.

The common denominator for all of these cadres is political clarity. This does not consist of unthinking support for the postulates of the revolution, but a reasoned support. It requires great capacity for sacrifice and a capacity for dialectical analysis, which will enable them to make continuous contributions on all levels to the rich theory and practice of the revolution. These compañeros should be selected from the masses solely by application of the principle that the best will come to the fore and that the best should be given the greatest opportunities for development.

In all these situations, the function of the cadre is the same, on each of the different fronts. The cadre is the key component of the ideological motor that is the United Party of the Revolution. It is something that we could call the dynamic gear of that motor. A gear inasmuch as he is a working part of the motor, making sure it works right. Dynamic inasmuch as he is not simply a transmitter of slogans or demands upward or downward, but a creator who will aid in the development of the masses and the information of the leaders, serving as a point of contact between them. The cadre has the important mission of seeing to it that the great spirit of the revolution is not dissipated, that it will not become dormant nor slacken its rhythm. It is a sensitive position. He transmits what comes from the masses and instills in the masses the party's orientation.

Therefore, the development of cadres is now a task that cannot be postponed. The development of cadres has been undertaken with great determination by the revolutionary government with its programs of scholarships based on the principles of selection; with its programs of study for workers, offering various opportunities for technological development; with the development of the special technical schools; with the development of secondary schools and universities, opening new careers. It has been done, in short, with the development of study, work, and revolutionary vigilance as watchwords for our entire country, fundamentally based on the Union of Young Communists, from which all types of cadres should emerge in the future, even the leading cadres of the revolution.

Intimately linked to the concept of "cadre" is the concept of capacity for sacrifice, for demonstrating through personal example the truths and watchwords of the revolution. The cadres, as political leaders, should gain the respect of the workers by their actions. It is absolutely imperative that they have the respect and affection of their compañeros, whom they must guide along the vanguard paths.

Because of all this, there are no better cadres than those chosen by the masses in the assemblies that select the exemplary workers, those who will join the PURS along with the old members of the ORI who pass all the required tests of selection. At the beginning they will constitute a small party, but with enormous influence among the workers. Later it will grow when the advance of socialist consciousness begins making work and total devotion to the cause of the people into a necessity. With intermediate leaders of this quality, the difficult tasks that we have before us will be accomplished with fewer mistakes. After a period of confusion and poor methods, we have arrived at a correct policy that will never be abandoned. With the ever-renewed impulse of the working class nourishing from its inexhaustible fountain the ranks of the future United Party of the Socialist Revolution, and with the leadership of our party, we fully undertake the task of forming cadres, who will guarantee the vigorous development of our revolution. We must triumph in this effort.

May Day speech

In Havana the May Day celebration begins the night before, and a speech at that time by Guevara soon became a tradition. The selections below are from his speech of April 30, 1963, at the García Lorca Theater. The meeting, honoring Cuba's outstanding workers and technicians for the year 1962, was held under the joint auspices of the Cuban Confederation of Labor–Revolutionary (CTC-R) and the Ministry of Industry, which Guevara headed.

Compañeros:

We meet once again, on the eve of the International Workers Festival, to honor those compañeros who by their efforts in the service of production for our country, and in the service of the noble cause of building socialism, have distinguished themselves as vanguard workers in each of the different enterprises into which our ministry is divided.

During the twelve months of the past year, we have held periodic talks with those compañeros who, by their dedication to work, month by month excelled among all the workers in our enterprises.

We have repeated over and over that, in the case of vanguard workers, excessive modesty is not a virtue but a defect; that the vanguard worker must show his example, make it vivid and palpable, communicate it, spread it far and wide. He must make his enthusiasm contagious to all the other compañeros, and see to it that his individual effort is transformed into a great, united, collective effort of all the workers. He must help transform the efforts of the vanguard factories into the great collective effort of all the factories of the country, of all the centers of production. He must see to it that simultaneously there is a deepening of both efficiency at work and the consciousness of our people, in order to obtain both the material abundance needed for the construction of socialism and the indestructible strength of consciousness of the country's sons and daughters, which are also needed for its defense in difficult moments.

During an entire year these two tasks have been completely fulfilled. Not without defects, not without more or less serious missteps, not without mistakes, stumbles, backward steps in order to get back on the road. But with unquenchable enthusiasm and complete dedication to our task in 1962, we laid more solidly the foundations for our society. We contributed, too, to the development of revolutionary consciousness in the entire world when, confronted with the atomic threats of the Yankee invader, our entire people rose last October and November and gave an answer that without doubt will pass into history.

It was an example of how a people in revolution can confront the greatest dangers, even the threat of atomic destruction itself—a threat unknown to other societies in world history. And it was an example of how with revolutionary consciousness and determination to win, and the militant solidarity of all the countries of the socialist camp and of all free men throughout the world, a small people, living at the gates of the most aggressive and powerful imperialist power on earth, can triumph, can maintain its sovereignty, and, most importantly, continue building its own society.

The central task assigned to us, compañeros, in the trench of production, is to constantly continue building, no matter what dangers threaten or what difficulties have to be overcome. And this is the task we are developing and improving.

Each year that passes we do less badly at least; each year we learn from our own errors and the experience of other peoples. In this way we are forging the basis of what will be in the future a powerful, autonomous, self-supporting industry in this country, a country that will have to rely on its great agricultural riches based on the fertility of its soil, on its favorable climate, and on a relatively low population density. . . .

You all know the immense number of illiterates we had in Cuba. We are all witnesses, and in some form participants in that battle, as heroic as any other battle, which we fought against lack of culture, in this case illiteracy.

But illiteracy is only the extreme expression of a people's lack of culture. Whoever learns just to read and write has taken only the first step toward culture, but cannot yet contribute anything to it.

Modern technique is advancing by giant steps. In order to be a qualified technician in this country, very soon it will be necessary to have a speaking knowledge of more than one language; to be able to read technical books will require knowledge of more than one language, to learn how to read the technical specifications and directions in whatever language, since the capitalists have also produced a great deal in technology—and produced it very well—and it is necessary to know how to take advantage of all those experiences.

Raising skill levels then is a cardinal task of the government and of all the people and it must not be abandoned. Men and women, even when tired after work, must make the indispensable effort to study, even if only for an hour or half-hour a day, and in this way try to keep increasing their knowledge.

It is not important that in a few weeks or months the distance covered may seem small. This is a task of years, and a task that must never end. It is also a task that is very difficult for a beginner, for a worker of a certain age who can barely read and write. But to the degree that new knowledge is acquired, culture will cease to be a revolutionary duty, or something more or less painful that must be done to fulfill a revolutionary obligation, and will instead become a human need. And then it will cease to be an effort to continue the task of learning.

In this work tremendous efforts and a prodigious amount of society's goods have been consumed and will continue to be consumed. We believe that culture and public health are services on which we can never spend enough for our people. The more we can give, the better it will be for all. And so we will continue to give as much as possible.

But remember, the teachers who are giving instruction to the worker-students at the various levels of study are being kept out of production and therefore constitute a state expense that should be repaid to society by redoubled effort.

We must take up another burning question: the new wage scale and the work norms. These are two closely related points that we have been discussing for over a year.

I remember that on the eve of last May Day, in this very same theater, I apologized for not having finished this task. Today, in a certain sense, I should again apologize, although the task of organizing the wage scales and work norms is very far advanced. And next month, by the middle of the month, pilot tests will begin in the various enterprises, not only in our ministry, but in all branches of the economy.

We will be able to complete the methods for giving a single wage scale for skill levels in the whole country, and a more equitable pay remuneration. But we must emphasize something that is still confused. The new wage scale, with the corresponding norms to be applied, does not necessarily signify a wage increase, far from it.

We have explained that in the first branch where this was set up, in mining—and only in some of the mines—on account of the relatively low pay, the work norms and the wage scale meant substantial increases for the compañeros there. But it will not be equally so in all branches.

There are some groups of workers at present who are being paid in accordance with the level considered adequate now, and some others who receive more than that level.

We have also made clear that all those workers whose average wage is higher than the new average wage decreed will continue to receive the full wage they have been getting, but divided into two parts: one corresponding to his actual work plus a surplus reflecting their current pay. This is being done so as not to upset the budgets of those compañeros, who won this higher wage over the years and under different circumstances, during the development of the capitalist process with its corresponding anarchic relations of production.

However, all new entrants in those branches of production will be under the new wage scale, and one of the main points to be measured in increasing pay under the scale will be the worker's qualifications. This means that all workers who are satisfactorily fulfilling the standards of quality and quantity over a period of time, but who cannot ascend automatically under the wage scale since they are not part of a new group with a different wage level, will have the opportunity to raise their qualifications and enter a higher income group, raising their wages in this way.

So, individual qualifications will always be taken into account in considering each individual's wage.

All this will be explained by the minister of labor. There

will be preliminary discussions and a whole process of clarification, since this is a very complicated task in which the whole economy of the country is bound up. But I wanted to make sure it was understood that the new wage scale does not necessarily signify an increase in pay.

In some cases, it will mean an increase in order to correct very low wages; in others, wages will remain the same, in accordance with standards adopted from the new studies. In still others, they will remain the same—but these compañeros will have a divided wage, although the basic amount will not be touched.

This will be done simply so that it will be clearly established that one part of the wage he is receiving belongs to him, let us say, for historical reasons, but that it is his individual wage. When this worker leaves his position, the wage for that job reverts to the norm, to the fixed basic wage, and not to the actual wage this hypothetical worker had been receiving. . . .

To finish this speech—a little long, a little tedious—I wanted to remind you, compañeros, of the responsibility that we have, all of us, without exception.

Today we are here to salute our best workers, the vanguard workers. And we are also saluting delegations of workers who have come to visit us from all over the world. . . .

We are a showcase, a mirror into which all the peoples of the Americas can look, and we must work to make our successes greater every day, and our failures fewer.

We must not return to the practice of hiding our defects so they aren't seen. That would neither be honest nor revolutionary. They will learn from our mistakes, as well. The compañeros from Latin America and the other countries of Asia and Africa who are fighting today for their independence will learn from our errors, too. We must not hide a single one of our errors, not a single one of the vices of the past that we have not yet been able to resolve, nor a single one of the errors we have made in the socialist present.

We must be open, because that is our duty, which reaches immense heights at this moment. And each of us is responsible to the peoples of the world for what the Cuban revolution does and will do.

Our path is not simple; it is full of danger and difficulties. Imperialism is lying in wait at every bend of the road, hoping for a moment of weakness in order to launch itself against us. The reactionaries of all Latin America are waiting to publish with joy even our own official acknowledgments of our errors.

Fundamentally they are trying to show Latin America and the whole world that if a small country such as ours, without industries, without technological development, tries to make a revolution, it is bound to fail. They use data and they use tricks—and they also use saboteurs and divisionists—to hold back our development.

We cannot allow ourselves a single moment of weakness. Not now, when we are directly under the visual inspection of our guests, nor at any time; for in each minute of our country's life we are under the avid inspection of all the peoples of Latin America, who see in us a new hope of salvation, a new hope of redeeming themselves from their chains.

Let us show them the realities of the road we have taken, compañeros! Let us show them that not only are we capable of the feat of confronting, almost unarmed at one time, the armed force of the oligarchy; of developing our popular armies by capturing arms from the enemy, of confronting them on the field of battle, and of catalyzing the consciousness of the entire people of Cuba in order to convert them into a great vanguard army and to destroy the dictatorship!

Let us show that we are not only capable of preparing our whole people to stand as one, to launch our war cry, our defiant shout that we all know. Let us also show, compañeros, that we are capable of emerging triumphant in this long, tiring, terrible struggle, through which we are building socialism in the midst of an imperialist blockade.

In the face of all the dangers, the threats and aggressions, the blockades, the sabotage, all the divisionists, all those powers who try to slow us down, we must show once more our people's capacity to make their own history.

We must all be united, compañeros, firm in our faith, firmer than ever today, though perhaps not so firm as we shall be tomorrow, to go forward always with our eyes on the future, with our feet on the ground, building what is ours at each step, and making sure of each step we take, so that we will never give up one inch of what we have won, of what we have built, of what is ours: socialism!

Patria o muerte! [Homeland or death]

Venceremos! [We shall win]

Guerrilla warfare: a method

Guevara's name is indissolubly linked with guerrilla warfare—in practice as well as theory. In Mexico he had been the outstanding student in the training that preceded embarkation on the *Granma*. In the Sierra Maestra he had risen to the rank of *comandante* (major), the highest conferred in the Rebel Army. His most celebrated book was *Guerrilla Warfare*. And, of course, he met his death in the course of the guerrilla fighting in Bolivia. The following is the complete text of his article, "Guerrilla Warfare: A Method," in *Cuba Socialista* of September 1963.

Guerrilla warfare has been employed on innumerable occasions throughout history in different circumstances, to achieve different aims. Of late it has been used in various people's wars of liberation when the vanguard of the people chose the path of irregular armed struggle against enemies of greater military power. Asia, Africa, and America have been the scene of such actions in an effort to attain power in the struggle against feudal, neocolonial, or colonial exploitation. In Europe, guerrilla warfare was used as a supplement to their own, or allied, regular armies.

Guerrilla warfare has been waged many times in Latin America. As a case in point closer to home, the experience of Augusto César Sandino fighting against the U.S. expeditionary force in the Segovia mountains of Nicaragua can be noted, and recently Cuba's revolutionary war. Since then in Latin America the questions of guerrilla warfare have been raised for theoretical discussions by the continent's progressive parties, and whether it is possible or expedient to use it, has become the subject of heated polemics.

This article will try to present our views on guerrilla warfare and its correct use.

Above all, it must be made clear that this form of struggle is a means—a means to an end. That end, essential and inevitable for every revolutionary, is the conquest of political power. Therefore, in analyzing specific situations in different countries of Latin America, one must employ the concept of guerrilla warfare in the limited sense of a method of struggle in order to gain that end.

Almost immediately the question arises: Is guerrilla warfare the only formula for seizing power in the whole of Latin America? Or at least will it be the predominant form? Or will it simply be one of many forms used in the struggle? In the final analysis it may be asked: Will the example of Cuba be applicable to other realities on the continent? In the course of polemics those who advocate guerrilla warfare are often criticized for forgetting mass struggle, almost as if these were counterposed methods. We reject this implication. Guerrilla warfare is a people's war, a mass struggle. To try to carry out this type of war without the support of the population is to court inevitable disaster. The guerrillas are the fighting vanguard of the people, stationed in a specified place in a certain territory, armed and prepared to carry out a series of military actions directed toward a single strategic end—the seizure of power. They have the support of the worker and peasant masses of the region and of the whole territory in which they operate. Without these prerequisites no guerrilla warfare is possible.

> We believe that the Cuban revolution made three fundamental contributions to the workings of the revolutionary movement in Latin America. They are: Firstly, popular forces can win a war against the army. Secondly, it's not always necessary to wait for all the revolutionary conditions to be present; the insurrectional movement itself can create them. Thirdly, in underdeveloped Latin America the field for armed struggle must fundamentally be the countryside. *(Guerrilla Warfare)*

Such are the contributions to the development of the revolutionary struggle in Latin America, and they can be applied to any of the countries on our continent where guerrilla warfare may be developed.

The *Second Declaration of Havana* points out:

> In our countries two circumstances are combined: underdeveloped industry and a feudal agrarian system. That is why no matter how hard the living conditions of the urban workers are, the rural population lives under even more horrible conditions of oppression and exploitation. But, with few exceptions, it also constitutes the absolute majority, sometimes more than 70 percent of the population in Latin America.
>
> Not counting the landlords who often live in the cities, the rest of this great mass earns its livelihood by working as peons on the plantations for the most miserable wages, or they work the soil under conditions of exploitation hardly distinguishable from those of the Middle Ages.
>
> These are the circumstances which determine that in

Latin America the poor population of the countryside constitutes a tremendous potential revolutionary force.

The armies on which the power of the exploiting classes rest, are structured and equipped for conventional warfare. They are the force upholding the power of the exploiting classes. But when they are confronted with the irregular warfare of peasants based on their own home grounds, they become absolutely powerless; they lose ten men for every revolutionary combatant who falls. Demoralization among them mounts rapidly when they are confronted by an invisible and invincible enemy that provides them no chance to display their military-academy tactics and their swaggering, which they use so much in military displays, to repress the workers and students in the cities.

The initial struggle of small fighting units is constantly nurtured by new forces; the mass movement begins to break out, little by little the old order breaks up into a thousand pieces and that is when the working class and the urban masses decide the battle.

What is it that, from the very beginning of the struggle, makes those units invincible, regardless of the number, strength, and resources of their enemies? It is the people's support, a support they can count on more and more.

But the peasantry is a class that, because of the ignorance in which it has been kept and the isolation in which it lives, requires the revolutionary and political leadership of the working class and revolutionary intellectuals. Without that it alone cannot launch the struggle and achieve victory.

In the present historical conditions of Latin America the national bourgeoisie cannot lead the antifeudal and anti-imperialist struggle. Experience demonstrates that in our nations this class—even when its interests clash with those of Yankee imperialism—has been incapable of confronting imperialism, paralyzed by fear of social revolution and frightened by the clamor of the exploited masses.

Supplementing these statements, which constitute the essence of the revolutionary declaration in Latin America, the *Second Declaration of Havana* in other paragraphs states the following:

> The subjective conditions in each country, the factors of consciousness, of organization, of leadership, can accelerate or delay the revolution, depending on the state of their development. But sooner or later, in each historic epoch, as objective conditions ripen, consciousness is acquired, organization is achieved, leadership arises, and the revolution is produced.
>
> Whether this takes place peacefully or comes to the world after painful birth pangs, does not depend on the revolutionaries; it depends on the reactionary forces of the old society, who resist allowing the new society to be born, a society produced by the contradictions within the old society itself. Revolution, in history, is like the doctor who assists at the birth of a new life: it does not use forceps unless it is necessary, but it will use them without hesitation whenever they are necessary to help in giving birth. Birth pangs bring the hope of a better life to the enslaved and exploited masses.
>
> Revolution is inevitable in many countries of Latin America today. Nobody's will determines this fact. It is determined by the frightful conditions of exploitation in which mankind lives in Latin America. It is determined by the development of the revolutionary consciousness of the masses, by the world crisis of imperialism, and by the universal movement of struggle of the world's subjugated peoples.

We shall start from this basis to analyze the whole question of guerrilla warfare in Latin America.

We have made clear that it is a means of struggle to achieve an end. Our first concern is to analyze the end and to see whether the conquest of power here in Latin America can be achieved in any other way than by armed struggle.

Peaceful struggle can be carried out through mass movements and can—in special situations of crisis—compel governments to yield, so that the popular forces eventually take power and establish a proletarian dictatorship. Theoretically this is correct. When analyzing this on the Latin American scene we must arrive at the following conclusions: Generally speaking, on this continent objective conditions exist that impel the masses to violent actions against the bourgeois and landlord governments. In many other countries crises of power and certain subjective conditions exist, too. Obviously, in the countries where all these conditions are present, it would be criminal not to act to seize power. In others where this situation does not occur, it is right that different alternatives should emerge and that the decision applicable to each country should come out of theoretical discussion. The only thing history does not permit is for the analysts and executors of proletarian policy to be wrong. No one can claim the role of vanguard party as if it were a university diploma. To be a vanguard party means to stand in the forefront of the working class in the struggle for the seizure of power, to know how to guide this struggle to success, including by short cuts. That is the mission of our revolutionary parties, and the analysis should be profound and exhaustive so that there are no mistakes.

At present in Latin America one sees a state of unstable equilibrium between oligarchical dictatorship and popular pressure. By "oligarchical" we mean the reactionary alliance between the bourgeoisie and the landlord class of each country with a greater or lesser preponderance of feudal structures. These dictatorships function within certain frameworks of legality, which they set up for themselves to facilitate their work during the whole unrestricted period of their class domination. At present, however, we are undergoing a stage in which the pressure of the people is very strong. They are knocking at the doors of bourgeois legality, which its own authors have to violate in order to check the impetus of the masses. The barefaced violations of all established legislation—or of legislation instituted subsequently to sanction their deeds—only heighten the tension of the people's forces. The oligarchical dictatorship, therefore, tries to utilize the old legal order to change the constitution and further suppress the proletariat without a head-on clash. Here is where a contradiction arises, however. The people can no longer tolerate the old, still less the new, coercive measures adopted by the dictatorship, and try to smash them. We must never forget the authoritarian and restrictive class character of the bourgeois state. Lenin refers to it in this way:

> The state is a product and a manifestation of the irreconcilability of class antagonisms. The state arises where, when, and insofar as class antagonisms objectively *cannot* be reconciled. And, conversely, the existence of the state proves that the class antagonisms are irreconcilable. *(State and Revolution)*

In other words, we must not allow the word "democracy," used in an apologetic manner to represent the dictatorship of the exploiting classes, to lose its deeper meaning and acquire the meaning of giving the people a more or less optimal set of liberties. To struggle only to restore a certain degree of bourgeois legality, without at the same time raising the question of revolutionary power, is to struggle for the return of a certain dictatorial order established by the dominant social classes. It is a struggle only for a lighter ball to be fixed to the convict's chains.

In these conditions of conflict, the oligarchy breaks its own contracts, its own mask of "democracy," and attacks the people, although it always tries to make use of the superstructure it has formed for oppression. At that moment, the question again arises: What is to be done? Our answer is: Violence is not the sole patrimony of the exploiters; the exploited can use it too, and what is more, they *should* use it at the opportune moment. Martí said: "He who wages war in a country that can avoid it is a criminal; so too is he who fails to wage a war that cannot be avoided."

And Lenin said:

> Social-Democracy has never taken a sentimental view of war. It unreservedly condemns war as a bestial means of settling conflicts in human society. But Social-Democracy knows that so long as society is divided into classes, so long as there is exploitation of man by man, wars are inevitable. This exploitation cannot be destroyed without war, and war is always and everywhere begun by the exploiters, by the ruling and oppressing classes.

He said this in 1905. Later, in "The War Program of the Proletarian Revolution," in a profound analysis of the nature of class struggle, he affirmed:

> He who accepts the class struggle cannot fail to accept civil wars, which in every class society are the natural, and under certain conditions inevitable, continuation, development and intensification of the class struggle. That has been confirmed by every great revolution. To repudiate civil war, or to forget about it, is to fall into extreme opportunism and renounce the socialist revolution.

That is to say, we should not be afraid of violence, the midwife of new societies. The only thing is that such violence should be unleashed at the precise moment when the people's leaders find circumstances most favorable.

What will these be? Subjectively, they depend upon two factors that are complementary and that in turn deepen in the course of the struggle: the consciousness of the need for change and the certainty of the possibility of this revolutionary change. These two factors, coupled with the objective conditions—which in nearly all of Latin America are highly favorable for the development of the struggle—with the firm will to attain it as well as the new relationship of forces in the world, determine the form of action.

However far away the socialist countries may be, their favorable influence will make itself felt among the fighting peoples who will be given more strength by their enlightening example. On July 26 of this year [1963], Fidel Castro said:

> The duty of revolutionaries, especially at this moment, is to know how to recognize and grasp the changes in the relationship of forces that have taken place in the world, and to understand that these changes facilitate the struggle of the peoples. The duty of revolutionaries, of Latin American revolutionaries, is not to wait for a change in the relationship of forces to produce the miracle of social revolutions in Latin America, but to take full advantage of everything in it that is favorable to the revolutionary movement—and to make revolutions!

There are people who say: "We admit that in certain specific cases revolutionary war is the appropriate way to attain political power; but where can we find those great leaders, the Fidel Castros who will lead us to victory?" Fidel Castro, like every human being, is a product of history. The military and political leaders, merged if possible into a single person, who will lead insurrectional struggles in Latin America, will learn the art of war in the exercise of war itself. There is no job or profession that can be learned from textbooks alone. In this case, struggle is the great teacher.

Naturally the task is not simple, nor is it exempt from serious threats all along the way.

During the development of the armed struggle there are two moments of extreme danger for the future of the revolution. The first of these arises in the preparatory stage and the way it is dealt with gives the measure of the determination for struggle and the clarity of purpose of the popular forces. When the bourgeois state advances against the positions of the people, there inevitably emerges a process of defense against the enemy who attacks at this moment of superiority. If the minimum subjective and objective conditions have already been developed, the defense must be armed, but not in such a way that the popular forces become mere recipients of the enemy's blows; nor should the stage of armed defense simply be transformed into a last refuge for the pursued. Guerrilla fighting, though at a given moment it may be a defensive movement of the people, carries within itself the capacity to attack the enemy and this quality must constantly be developed. This capacity is what determines, as time goes on, the catalytic character of the popular forces. That is to say, guerrilla fighting is not passive self-defense; it is defense with attack, and from the moment it is recognized as such, it has as a final perspective the conquest of political power.

This moment is important. In social processes the difference between violence and nonviolence cannot be measured by the number of shots exchanged; it depends on concrete and fluctuating situations. And one must know how to recognize the exact moment when the popular forces, conscious of their relative weakness but at the same time of their strategic strength, should take the initiative so that the situation does not recede. The equilibrium between the oligarchic dictatorship and the pressure of the people must be upset. The dictatorship constantly tries to function without resorting to force. Being obliged to appear without disguise, that is to say, in its true aspect as a violent dictatorship of the reactionary classes, will contribute to its unmasking, and this will deepen the struggle to such an extent that it will not be able to be turned back. The resolute beginning of long-range armed action depends on how the people's forces fulfill their function, which amounts to the task of forcing a decision on the dictatorship—to draw back or to unleash the struggle.

Avoiding the other moment of danger depends on the ability to develop the growth of the popular forces. Marx always advised that once the revolutionary process has begun, the proletariat must strike and strike without letup. A revolution that does not constantly deepen is a revolution going backward. The combatants, once wearied, begin to lose faith, and then some of the bourgeois maneuvers to which we have been so accustomed may bear fruit. These can be the holding of elections to hand the government over to some other gentleman with a more honeyed voice and a more angelic face than the outgoing dictator, or the staging of a coup by reactionaries, generally headed by the army and supported, directly or indirectly, by progressive forces. There are other maneuvers as well, but it is not our intention to analyze tactical stratagems.

Let us focus our main attention on the operation of the military coup mentioned above. What can leaders of the military contribute to true democracy? What kind of loyalty can be asked of them, if they are mere instruments of domination by the reactionary classes and imperialist monopolies and, as a caste whose worth rests only on the weapons in their hands, they aspire only to maintain their prerogatives?

When, in situations difficult for the oppressors, the military men conspire to overthrow a dictator who in fact is finished, it can be assumed that they do so because the dictator is unable to preserve their class prerogatives without extreme violence, something that in general does not serve the interests of the oligarchies at that moment.

This statement does not in any sense mean rejecting the services of military men as individual fighters who, separated from the society they have served, have in fact rebelled against it. They should be made use of in accordance with the revolutionary line they adopt as fighters and not as representatives of a caste.

Long ago, Engels, in the preface to the third edition of *The Civil War in France*, remarked:

> The workers were armed after every revolution; ". . . therefore the disarming of the workers was the first commandment for the bourgeois, who were at the helm of the state. Hence, after every revolution won by the workers, a new struggle, ending with the defeat of the workers." (Quoted by Lenin in *State and Revolution*)

This play of continuous struggles in which some formal change is brought about and then strategically withdrawn, has been repeated for decades in the capitalist world. But even worse, the continuous deception of the proletariat along these lines has been practiced periodically for more than a century.

There is also a danger that the leaders of the progressive parties, desiring to prolong conditions more favorable for revolutionary action by using certain aspects of bourgeois legality, lose sight of the goal, something that is very common in the course of action, and forget the definitive strategic objective: *the seizure of power.*

These two difficult moments of the revolution that we

have briefly analyzed can be surmounted when the Marxist-Leninist party leaders are capable of clearly seeing the implications of the moment and of mobilizing the masses to the maximum, leading them onto the correct path of resolving fundamental contradictions.

In elaborating these ideas, we have assumed that eventually the idea of armed struggle as well as the formula of guerrilla warfare as a method of fighting will be accepted. Why do we think that guerrilla warfare is the correct way in the present situation in Latin America? There are fundamental arguments that in our opinion determine the necessity of guerrilla action as the central axis of the struggle in Latin America.

First, accepting as true that the enemy will fight to maintain itself in power, it is necessary to have in view the destruction of the oppressor army. To do this, it is necessary to confront it with a popular army. Such an army is not born spontaneously; it must be armed from the enemy's arsenal and this demands a very long and very hard struggle in which the popular forces and their leaders will always be exposed to attack by superior forces and be without adequate conditions of defense and maneuverability.

On the other hand, the guerrilla nucleus, established in areas favorable to the struggle, ensures the security and continuity of the revolutionary command. The urban forces commanded by the general staff of the people's army can perform actions of the utmost importance. But the eventual destruction of these groups would not kill the soul of the revolution, its leadership. This would continue to spark the revolutionary spirit of the masses from its rural stronghold, organizing new forces for other battles.

Moreover, the construction of the future state apparatus begins in this area, an apparatus entrusted with leading the class dictatorship efficiently during the whole period of transition. The longer the struggle, the greater and more complicated the administrative problems, and to solve them cadres will be trained for the difficult task of consolidating power and economic development at a later stage.

Secondly, the general situation of the Latin American peasantry and the increasingly explosive character of its struggle against feudal structures in the framework of an alliance between local and foreign exploiters.

Returning to *The Second Declaration of Havana:*

> At the outset of the past century, the peoples of Latin America freed themselves from Spanish colonialism, but they did not free themselves from exploitation. The feudal landlords assumed the authority of the governing Spaniards, the Indians continued in their painful servitude, the Latin American remained a slave in one form or another, and the minimum hopes of the peoples died under the power of the oligarchies and the tyranny of foreign capital. This is the truth of Latin America, with one or another degree of variation or shading. Latin America today is under a much more ferocious imperialism, more powerful and ruthless than the Spanish colonial empire.
>
> What is Yankee imperialism's attitude in face of the objective and historically inexorable reality of the Latin American revolution? To prepare to unleash a colonial war against the peoples of Latin America; to create an apparatus of force, the political pretexts, and the pseudolegal instruments underwritten by the representatives of the reactionary oligarchies, in order to repress, by blood and by iron, the struggle of the Latin American peoples.

This objective situation demonstrates the latent, unused strength in our peasants and the need to utilize it for the liberation of Latin America.

Thirdly, the continental character of the struggle.

Could this new stage of the emancipation of Latin America be conceived as a confrontation of two local forces struggling for power in a given territory? Hardly. It will be a struggle to the death between all the forces of the people and all the forces of repression. This too is forecast by the passages quoted above.

The Yankees will intervene out of solidarity of interests and because the struggle in Latin America is decisive. In fact, they are already intervening in the preparation of repressive forces and the organization of a continental apparatus of struggle. But from now on they will do so with all their energy; they will strike at the people's forces with all the weapons of destruction at their disposal. They will try to prevent the consolidation of revolutionary power; and if it should be successful anywhere, they will renew their attack. They will not recognize it. They will try to divide the revolutionary forces. They will introduce all types of saboteurs, create border incidents, engage other reactionary states to oppose it, and will try to strangle the new state economically—in a word, to annihilate it.

This being the picture in Latin America, it is difficult to achieve and consolidate victory in an isolated country. The unity of the repressive forces must encounter the unity of the popular forces. In all the countries in which oppression reaches unbearable proportions, the banner of rebellion must be raised, and this banner of historical necessity will have a continental character. As Fidel said, the mountain chain of the Andes is destined to become the Sierra Maestra of the Americas, and all the immense territories that make up this continent are destined to become the scene of a life-and-death struggle against the power of imperialism.

We cannot say when this struggle will acquire continental characteristics nor how long it will last; but we can predict its approach and its triumph, because it is the inevitable result of historical, economic, and political conditions and its course cannot be turned back. It is the task of the revolutionary force in each country to initiate it when the conditions are present, regardless of the situation in other countries. The general strategy will emerge as the struggle develops. The prediction on the continental character of the struggle is the result of an analysis of the strength of each contender, but this does not in the least exclude independent outbreaks. Just as the beginning of the struggle in one part of a country is bound to develop the struggle throughout its territory, the beginning of a revolutionary war contributes to the development of new conditions in the neighboring countries.

The development of revolutions has normally produced high and low tides in inverse proportion: to the revolutionary high tide corresponds the counterrevolutionary low tide; and conversely, at moments of revolutionary decline, there is a counterrevolutionary ascendency. At such moments the situation of the popular forces becomes difficult, and they should resort to the best defensive measures in order to suffer the fewest losses. The enemy is extremely powerful on a continental level. Therefore the relative weaknesses of the local bourgeoisie cannot be analyzed with a view to making decisions within a restricted area. Still less can one think of an eventual alliance of these oligarchies with an armed people. The Cuban revolution has sounded the alarm. The polarization of forces is becoming complete: exploiters on one side and exploited on the other. The mass of the petty bourgeoisie will lean to one side or the other in accordance with their interests and the political skill with which it is treated; neutrality will be an exception. This is how revolutionary war will be.

Let us consider the way a guerrilla center can start.

Nuclei of relatively few persons choose places favorable for guerrilla warfare, sometimes with the intention of launching a counterattack or to weather a storm, and there they begin action. But the following must be made clear: At the beginning, the relative weakness of the guerrilla force is such that its actions in an area should be carried out only for the purposes of becoming acquainted with the surroundings, establishing connections with the population, and fortifying the places that eventually will be converted into its bases.

A guerrilla unit can survive only if it starts by basing its development on the three following conditions: constant mobility, constant vigilance, and constant wariness. Without the adequate use of these elements of military tactics, the unit will find it hard to survive. It must be remembered that the heroism of the guerrilla fighter at such times consists in the scope of the planned objective and the long series of sacrifices that must be made in order to attain it.

These sacrifices will not mean daily combat or face-to-face struggle with the enemy; they will assume forms more subtle and difficult for the individual guerrilla fighter to endure physically and mentally.

The guerrillas will perhaps suffer heavily from the attacks of enemy armies. At times they will be split up, while those taken prisoner will be martyred. They will be pursued like hunted animals in the areas they have chosen to operate in, with the constant anxiety of having the enemy on their track. On top of all this they will have constant wariness to everything, since in some cases the terrorized peasants will give them away to the repressive troops in order to save their own skins. They have no alternative but death or victory at times when death is a concept a thousand times present, and victory a myth only a revolutionary can dream of.

That is the heroism of the guerrilla. That is why it is also said that to be on the march is one form of combat, while avoiding battle at a given moment is another form of combat. Faced with the general superiority of the enemy, the way to act is to find a form of tactics with which to gain a relative superiority at a chosen point, either by being able to concentrate more troops than the enemy or by making the best use of the terrain to secure advantages that upset the relationship of forces. In these conditions tactical victory is assured; if relative superiority is not clear, it is preferable not to take action. As long as one is in a position to choose the "how" and the "when," no battle should be fought that will not end in victory.

Guerrilla forces will grow and be consolidated within the framework of the great political and military action of which they are a part. And within this framework they will go on forming the bases, which are essential to the success of a guerrilla army. These bases are points that the enemy can penetrate only at the cost of heavy losses; they are bastions of the revolution, both shelters and staging grounds for bolder and increasingly more distant raids by the guerrilla force.

Such a time will come if the tactical and political difficulties have been simultaneously overcome. The guerrillas must never forget their function as vanguard of the people, the mandate they embody, and therefore they should create the necessary political conditions for the establishment of revolutionary power based on the full support of the masses. The main demands of the peasantry should be met to the degree and in the form that circumstances permit, making the entire population into a compact and determined body.

If the military situation is difficult from the first moments, the political situation will be no less delicate. If a single military error can wipe out the guerrillas, a political error can check their development for a long period.

The struggle is political and military; so it must develop, and so it must be understood.

In the course of its growth the guerrilla force reaches a point at which its capacity for action covers a given region, for which there are too many men and too great a concentration. Then begins the beehive action, in which one of the commanding officers, a distinguished guerrilla, heads off to another region and repeats the chain development of guerrilla warfare, but still subject to a central command.

It is necessary to point out that one cannot hope for victory without the formation of a popular army. The guerrilla forces can be expanded to a certain size; the popular forces, in the cities and in other enemy-occupied zones, can inflict losses, but the military potential of reaction would remain intact. It must always be remembered that the final outcome should be the annihilation of the enemy. Therefore all these new zones that have been created, as well as the penetrated zones behind the enemy lines and the forces operating in the principal cities, should be under a unified command. It cannot be claimed that this would be the strict hierarchy of command that characterizes an army, but it would be a strategic command structure. Within certain conditions of freedom of action, the guerrillas should carry out all the strategic orders of the central command, set up in one of the most secure and strongest areas, preparing conditions for the union of the forces at a given moment.

The guerrilla war, or war of liberation, will generally have three stages: First, the strategic defensive, when a small force hits at the enemy and makes off, not to find shelter in passive defense within a small circumference, but rather to defend itself by limited attacks it is able to carry out. After this comes a state of equilibrium, during which the possibilities of action on the part of both the enemy and the guerrillas are established. Then comes the final stage of overrunning the repressive army, ending in the capture of the big cities, in large-scale decisive encounters, and in the total annihilation of the enemy.

After reaching a state of equilibrium, when both sides are on guard against each other, in the ensuing development guerrilla warfare acquires new characteristics. The concept of maneuver is introduced with large columns attacking strong points, and a war of movement with the shifting of forces and of considerable means of attack. But owing to the capacity of resistance and counterattack that the enemy still retains, this war of maneuver does not entirely replace guerrilla fighting; it is only one form of action taken by the larger guerrilla forces until finally they crystallize into a popular army with army corps. Even at this time, the guerrillas will still utilize guerrilla methods properly speaking, moving ahead of the actions of the main forces, destroying communications and sabotaging the enemy's whole defensive apparatus.

We have predicted that the war will be continental. This means it will be protracted; it will have many fronts, and will cost much blood and countless lives over a long period. But it will have an additional result: the phenomena of polarization of forces occurring in Latin America, the clear division between exploiters and exploited that will exist in future revolutionary wars, means that when the armed vanguard of the people seizes power, the country or countries that attain it will simultaneouly have liquidated both the imperialists and the national exploiters. The first stage of the socialist revolution will have crystallized; the people will be ready to staunch their wounds and begin to build socialism.

Will there be other, less bloody, possibilities?

Some time ago, there occurred the last dividing up of the world, in which the United States took the lion's share of our continent; today the imperialists of the Old World are developing anew, and the might of the European Common Market is threatening the United States itself. All this might lead to the belief that it will be possible to watch the interimperialist struggle as spectators in order to attain further advances, perhaps in alliance with the strongest national bourgeoisies. Apart from the consideration that in class struggle a passive policy never brings good results and that alliances with the bourgeoisie, however revolutionary they may appear at a given moment, have only a transitory character, the time factor will induce us to take another path. The sharpening of the fundamental contradiction in Latin America appears to be so rapid that it upsets the "normal" development of contradictions within the imperialist camp in their struggle over markets.

The national bourgeoisies for the most part have united with U.S. imperialism and must share the same fate in each country. Even cases of agreements or common contradictions between the national bourgeoisie and other imperialists in opposition to U.S. imperialism occur within the framework of a fundamental struggle that in the course of its development inevitably embraces *all the exploited and all the exploiters.* The polarization of antagonistic forces among class enemies is, up to the present, more rapid than the development of the contradictions among exploiters over the division of the spoils. There are two camps: the alternative becomes clearer for every individual and for every particular stratum of the population.

The Alliance for Progress is an attempt to check what cannot be checked.

But if the advance of the European Common Market, or any other imperialist group on Latin American markets, were to be more rapid than the development of the fundamental contradiction, it would only mean that the popular forces would have to be introduced as a wedge into the open breach, carrying on this whole struggle and utilizing the new intruders with a clear awareneses of their final intentions.

Not a single position, not a single weapon, not a single secret, should be given up to the class enemy, under penalty of losing all.

The eruption of the struggle in Latin America has in fact begun. Will its storm center be in Venezuela, Guatemala, Colombia, Peru, or Ecuador? Are these present skirmishes only a manifestation of a restlessness that has not come to fruition?

It does not matter what the result of today's struggles will be. It does not matter, so far as the final result is concerned, whether one or another movement is temporarily defeated. What is certain is the determination to struggle that ripens day by day, the consciousness of the need for revolutionary change, the certainty that it is possible.

This is a prediction. We make it with the conviction that history will prove us right. An analysis of the subjective and objective factors in Latin America and in the imperialist world points to the accuracy of these assertions based on *The Second Declaration of Havana.*

Camilo

On October 28, 1959, a plane carrying Camilo Cienfuegos, the most colorful of Castro's top commanders, from Camagüey to Havana disappeared. Despite an intense mass search led by Castro himself, no trace of the plane was found and it was presumed blown out to sea and lost. Cienfuegos had been one of Guevara's closest comrades, and the latter's book, *Guerrilla Warfare,* which appeared a few months later, bore a moving dedication to Camilo. Indeed, the four final paragraphs of the memorial piece below are repeated from that dedication.

Guevara wrote this piece in October 1964, for *Verde Olivo,* but then delayed its publication in order to work on it further and "produce something more serious." He never got to do that, and *Verde Olivo* published it in its issue devoted to Che's memory.

Memory is a way of reviving the past, of recalling the dead. To remember Camilo is to recall the past or the dead, and yet Camilo is a living part of the Cuban revolution, immortal by his very nature. I would simply like to give our comrades of the Rebel Army an idea of who this invincible guerrilla fighter was. I am able to do so since we were always together, from the sad hours of the first setback at Alegría de Pío on. And it is my duty to do so, because, more than a comrade in arms, in joys, and in victories, Camilo was in truth a brother.

I never got to know him in Mexico, as he joined us at the last minute. He had come from the United States without any previous recommendation, and there were doubts about him—and everyone else for that matter—in those risky days. He came on the *Granma,* as just one among the eighty-two who crossed the sea, at the mercy of the elements, to bring something new to the Americas.

I was introduced to Camilo before actually meeting him, through some words of his that became a symbol. It was at the moment of the disaster at Alegría de Pío. I was wounded, sprawled out in a clearing, and by my side was a comrade covered with blood who was firing his last rounds, ready to die fighting. I heard someone cry weakly: "We're lost. We must surrender." Then from somewhere came a forceful voice that seemed to me the voice of the people: "Nobody surrenders here! Hell no!"

Things happened, our lives were saved—mine thanks to the efforts of Comrade Almeida—and five of us wandered around the steep cliffs near Cabo Cruz. One clear, moonlit night we came upon three other comrades sleeping peacefully, without any fear of the soldiers. We jumped them, believing they were enemies. Nothing happened, but the incident served later as the material for a joke among us: the fact that I was among those who had caught them by surprise, and it was I who had to raise the white flag so that they would not shoot us, mistaking us for Batista's men.

The eight of us continued on. Camilo was hungry and wanted to eat; he didn't care what or where, he simply wanted to eat. This led to some serious disagreements with Camilo, because he continually wanted to approach peasant huts to ask for food. Twice, for having followed the advice of "the eaters," we nearly fell into the hands of the army that had killed dozens of our comrades. On the ninth day the "gluttonous" part of our group won out, and we approached a peasant hut, ate, and all got sick. And among the sickest was, naturally, Camilo, who like a hungry lion had gulped down an entire kid.

During that period I was more a medic than a combatant. I put Camilo on a special diet and ordered him to stay behind in the hut, where he would be guarded and receive proper attention. That trouble passed, and we were together again, and the days turned into weeks and months during which many comrades fell along the way. Camilo was showing his mettle, earning the rank of lieutenant of the forward detachment in our one and only beloved column, which would later be called the "José Martí" Column no. 1, under Fidel's personal command. Almeida and Raúl were captains; Camilo, lieutenant of the forward detachment; Efigenio Ameijeiras, lieutenant of the rear guard; Ramiro Valdés, lieutenant in one of Raúl's platoons; and Calixto, soldier in another platoon. In short, all our forces were born there, and I was the group's lieutenant medic. Later, following the battle of Uvero, I was given the rank of captain, and, a few days later, that of commander leading a column. Life went on, and one day Camilo was made captain of the column I commanded, Column no. 4. We bore that number to deceive the enemy, since it was actually only the second. And it was here that Camilo began his new career of exploits. With untiring effort and extraordinary zeal, he hunted down enemy soldiers time and again. Once he killed a soldier in the enemy's advance squad at such close range that he caught the man's rifle before it even hit the ground. Another time he planned to let the first of the enemy soldiers go by until they were level with our troop, and then open fire from the side. The ambush never materialized, because someone in our group got nervous and began firing before the enemy got close enough. By then Camilo had become "Camilo, Lord of the Vanguard," a complete guerrilla fighter who asserted himself through his own colorful way of fighting.

I recall my anxiety during the second attack on Pino del Agua, when Fidel ordered me to stay with him and gave Camilo the responsibility of attacking one of the enemy's flanks. The idea was simple. Camilo was to attack and take one end of the enemy camp and then lay siege. But when the hurricane of fire began, he and his men took the sentry post and continued advancing, entering the village, killing or taking prisoner every soldier in their path. The town was taken house by house until finally the enemy organized its resistance and the barrage of lead began to take its toll among our ranks. Valuable comrades, among them Noda and Capote, lost their lives there.

An enemy machine gunner advanced with his men, but at one point he found himself in the midst of a veritable storm of gunfire. With his assistants killed, the soldier dropped the gun and fled. It was already daybreak; the attack had begun at night. Camilo hurled himself at the machine gun to seize and defend it, and was shot twice. One bullet pierced his left thigh and another went through his abdomen. He got out of there, and his comrades carried him. We were two kilometers away, with the enemy between us. We could hear machine gun bursts and the enemy shouting: "There goes Camilo's gun!" "That's Camilo firing!" and cheers for Batista. We all thought Camilo had been killed. Later we praised his luck that the bullet had entered and left his abdomen without hitting his intestines or any vital organ.

Later came the tragic days of April 9, and Camilo, the trailblazer, went on to create his legend on the Oriente plains, striking terror in the hearts of the enemy forces mobilized in the Bayamo region. Once he was surrounded by six hundred soldiers, with only twenty men, and he resisted an entire day against the enemy's advance that included two tanks. At night they made a spectacular escape.

Then came the offensive, and in the face of imminent danger and the concentration of forces, Camilo was called back, as he was the man Fidel trusted to leave in his place when he went to a specific front.

Later came the marvelous story of the invasion and his chain of victories on the plains of Las Villas—a difficult feat, as the terrain afforded little natural protection. His actions were magnificent for their audacity, and at the same time one could already see Camilo's political sense, his decisions on revolutionary questions, his strength, and his faith in the people.

Camilo was happy, witty, and loved to joke. I remember that in the Sierra a peasant—one of our great, magnificent, anonymous heroes—had received a nickname from Camilo, who accompanied it with a disdainful look. One day the peasant came to see me as head of the column, complaining that he shouldn't be insulted and that he was no "ventriloquist." As I did not understand, I went to speak with Camilo to get an explanation of the man's strange behavior. It turned out that Camilo had looked at the man with a scornful air and called him a ventriloquist, and since the peasant didn't know what the word meant, he was terribly offended.

Camilo had a little alcohol burner, and he used to cook cats and offer them as a delicacy to new recruits who joined us. It was one of the many tests of the Sierra, and more than one failed this preliminary "examination" when he refused to eat the cat. Camilo was a man of anecdotes, a thousand anecdotes. They came naturally, in passing. His appreciation of people and his easygoing nature were a part of his personality. These qualities, which today we sometimes forget or overlook, stamped his character and were present in all his actions, something precious that few men can attain. It is true, as Fidel has said, that he had no great amount of "book learning," but he had the natural intelligence of the people, who had chosen him from among thousands to place him in that privileged place earned by his audacity, his perseverance, his intelligence, and his devotion. Camilo was devoted and loyal to two things, and with the same results: he had unlimited personal loyalty toward Fidel, and he was loyal and devoted to the people. The people and Fidel march as one, and Camilo's devotion was projected toward them both as one.

Who killed Camilo? Who physically eliminated the man who lives on in the people? Such men do not die so long as the people do not authorize it. The enemy killed him; they killed him because they wanted him to die, because there are no completely safe airplanes, because pilots are not able to acquire all the necessary experience, because he was overloaded with work and had to be in Havana as quickly as possible. He was killed by his personal characteristics. Camilo did not measure danger. He utilized it as a game, he played with it, he courted it, he attracted it, handled it, and with his guerrilla's mentality, a mere cloud could not detain or derail him from the line he was following. It happened at a time when everyone knew him, admired and loved him; it could have happened before, and then his story would have been simply that of a guerrilla captain.

There will be many Camilos, as Fidel said. And, I might add, there have been many Camilos—Camilos who died before completing their magnificent cycle that he managed to complete so as to enter the pages of history. Camilo and the other Camilos—the ones who never made it this far and those yet to come—they are the measure of the people's strength; they are the highest expression of what can be achieved by a nation fighting to defend its purest ideals and with complete faith in the fulfillment of its noblest goals.

There is too much to be said to allow me to put his essence

into a lifeless mold, which would be equivalent to killing him. It is better to leave it like this, in general descriptive terms, without spelling out in black and white his socioeconomic ideas, which were not precisely defined. But we must always bear in mind that there was never a man—not even before the revolution—comparable to Camilo: a complete revolutionary, a man of the people, an artist of the revolution, sprung from the heart of the Cuban nation. His mind was incapable of the slightest slackening or deception.

Camilo the guerrilla is a permanent object of daily remembrance; he is the one who did this or that, something by Camilo; he who left his exact and indelible imprint on the Cuban revolution, who is present among those who fell before the triumph and those heroes yet to come. In his constant and eternal rebirth, Camilo is the image of the people.

At the United Nations

In addition to being a military leader, President of the National Bank, and minister of industry, Guevara played an important role in Cuban diplomacy. In 1959 he made a tour of Afro-Asian countries; in 1960 he headed an economic delegation to the Soviet bloc countries, China, and North Korea; in 1961 he represented Cuba at Punta del Este; in 1962 he headed another economic mission to the Soviet Union; in 1963 he attended a conference on economic planning in Algeria; in March 1964, he represented Cuba at the United Nations Conference on Trade and Development in Geneva, then went to Algeria again on an official mission, made a third trip to the Soviet Union in November, and represented Cuba in the 19th Session of the UN General Assembly in New York. The following are excerpts from his speech to the UN on December 11, 1964.

. . . Cuba comes here to state its position on the most important points of controversy and will do so with the full sense of responsibility that the use of this rostrum implies, while at the same time fulfilling the unavoidable duty of speaking clearly and frankly.

We would like to see this assembly shake itself out of complacency and move forward. We would like to see the committees begin their work and not stop at the first confrontation. Imperialism wants to turn this meeting into a pointless oratorical tournament, instead of solving the serious problems of the world. We must prevent it from doing so. This session of the assembly should not be remembered in the future solely by the number nineteen that identifies it. Our efforts are directed to that end.

We feel that we have the right and the obligation to do so, because our country is one of the most constant points of friction. It is one of the places where the principles upholding the right of small countries to sovereignty are put to the test day by day, minute by minute. At the same time, our country is one of the trenches of freedom in the world, situated a few steps away from United States imperialism, showing by its actions, its daily example, that in the present conditions of humanity the peoples can liberate themselves and can keep themselves free.

Of course, there now exists a socialist camp that becomes stronger day by day and has more powerful weapons of struggle. But additional conditions are required for survival: the maintenance of internal unity, faith in one's own destiny, and the irrevocable decision to fight to the death for the defense of one's country and revolution. These conditions, distinguished delegates, exist in Cuba.

Of all the burning problems to be dealt with by this assembly, one of special significance for us, and one whose solution we feel must be found first—so as to leave no doubt in the minds of anyone—is that of peaceful coexistence among states with different economic and social systems. Much progress has been made in the world in this field. But imperialism, particularly U.S. imperialism, has attempted to make the world believe that peaceful coexistence is the exclusive right of the earth's great powers. We say here what our president said in Cairo, and what later was expressed in the declaration of the Second Conference of Heads of State or Government of Nonaligned Countries: that peaceful coexistence cannot be limited to the powerful countries if we want to ensure world peace. Peaceful coexistence must be exercised among all states, regardless of size, regardless of the previous historical relations that linked them, and regardless of the problems that may arise among some of them at a given moment. . . .

We must also state that it is not only in relations among sovereign states that the concept of peaceful coexistence needs to be precisely defined. As Marxists we have maintained that peaceful coexistence among nations does not encompass coexistence between the exploiters and the exploited, between the oppressors and the oppressed. . . .

We express our solidarity with the people of Puerto Rico and their great leader, Pedro Albizu Campos, who, in another act of hypocrisy, has been set free at the age of seventy-two, almost unable to speak, paralyzed, after spending a lifetime in jail. Albizu Campos is a symbol of the as yet unfree but indomitable Latin America. Years and years of prison, almost unbearable pressures in jail, mental torture, solitude, total isolation from his people and his family, the insolence of the conqueror and its lackeys in the land of his birth—nothing broke his will. The delegation of Cuba, on behalf of its people, pays a tribute of admiration and gratitude to a patriot who confers honor upon Our America.

The United States for many years has tried to convert Puerto Rico into a model of hybrid culture: the Spanish language with English inflections, the Spanish language with hinges on its backbone—the better to bow down before the Yankee soldier. Puerto Rican soldiers have been used as cannon fodder in imperialist wars, as in Korea, and have even been made to fire at their own brothers, as in the massacre perpetrated by the U.S. army a few months ago against the unarmed people of Panama—one of the most recent crimes carried out by Yankee imperialism. And yet, despite this assault on their will and their historical destiny, the people of Puerto Rico have preserved their culture, their Latin character, their national feelings, which in themselves give proof of the implacable desire for independence lying within the masses of that Latin American island. . . .

One of the fundamental themes of this conference is general and complete disarmament. We express our support for general and complete disarmament. Furthermore, we advocate the complete destruction of all thermonuclear devices and we support the holding of a conference of all the nations of the world to make this aspiration of all people a reality. In his statement before this assembly, our prime minister warned that arms races have always led to war. There are new nuclear powers in the world, and the possibilities of a confrontation are growing.

We believe that such a conference is necessary to obtain the total destruction of thermonuclear weapons and, as a first step, the total prohibition of tests. At the same time, we have to establish clearly the duty of all countries to respect the present borders of other states and to refrain from engaging in any aggression, even with conventional weapons.

In adding our voice to that of all the peoples of the world who ask for general and complete disarmament, the destruction of all nuclear arsenals, the complete halt to the building of new thermonuclear devices and of nuclear tests of any kind, we believe it necessary to also stress that the territorial integrity of nations must be respected and the armed hand of imperialism held back, for it is no less dangerous when it uses only conventional weapons. Those who murdered thousands of defenseless citizens of the Congo did not use the atomic bomb. They used conventional weapons.

Conventional weapons have also been used by imperialism, causing so many deaths. . . .

Cuba reaffirms once again the right to maintain on its territory the weapons it deems appropriate, and its refusal to recognize the right of any power on earth—no matter how powerful—to violate our soil, our territorial waters, or our airspace.

If in any assembly Cuba assumes obligations of a collective nature, it will fulfill them to the letter. So long as this does not happen, Cuba maintains all its rights, just as any other nation. In the face of the demands of imperialism, our prime minister laid out the five points necessary for the existence of a secure peace in the Caribbean.

They are:

1. A halt to the economic blockade and all economic and trade pressures by the United States, in all parts of the world, against our country.

2. A halt to all subversive activities, launching and landing of weapons and explosives by air and sea, organization of mercenary invasions, infiltration of spies and saboteurs, acts all carried out from the territory of the United States and some accomplice countries.

3. A halt to pirate attacks carried out from existing bases in the United States and Puerto Rico.

4. A halt to all the violations of our airspace and our territorial waters by United States aircraft and warships.

5. Withdrawal from the Guantánamo naval base and return of the Cuban territory occupied by the United States. . . .

Interview by Mrs. Josie Fanon

After the UN session, Guevara flew to Africa. While in Algiers, he granted the following interview to Mrs. Josie Fanon, widow of Frantz Fanon, author of *The Wretched of the Earth*. The interview appeared in the December 26, 1964, issue of *Révolution Africaine*.

JOSIE FANON: What is the reason for your visit to Algeria?

CHE GUEVARA: The reason for my visit is very simple. In a few days I am going to visit a number of African countries, and to go to Africa it is necessary for us to come to Algeria first. We are also utilizing the occasion, before we leave, to discuss general international and African problems with the compañeros of the Algerian government. Possibly we'll stay two or three days longer in Algeria.

JOSIE FANON: Would you indicate in broad outline the position of the Cuban government in relation to Africa as a whole?

CHE GUEVARA: Africa represents one of the most important, if not the most important, fields of battle against all forms of exploitation existing in the world, against imperialism, colonialism, and neocolonialism. There are great possibilities for success in Africa, but there are also many dangers. The positive aspects include the youth of the African peoples as modern states, the hatred that colonialism has left in the minds of the people, the very clear consciousness the peoples possess of the profound differences existing between an African man and the colonizer, the conviction that there can never be sincere friendship between them except after the definitive departure of the colonizer. There are also other positive aspects: the possibilities at present of a much more rapid development than even a few years ago due to the aid that the socialist countries can offer, as well as that which some of the capitalist countries can likewise provide under certain conditions (but on this point we must be vigilant).

What we consider to be the principal danger for Africa is the possibility of division among the African peoples, which appears to be continually increasing. On one side are the lackeys of imperialism, on the other are the peoples seeking the most appropriate methods to free themselves. We have concrete reasons for fearing this danger. There is the phenomenon of unequal exchange between the industrialized countries and the economically dependent countries. This relation of inequality is shown in the most brutal way in connection with colonialism. But the completely independent countries also risk finding themselves locked up in the prison of the capitalist market because the big industrialized countries impose this through their high technical development. The big developed countries begin, after independence, to exercise a kind of "suction" on the liberated countries, and after a few years the conditions are again ripe for political and economic domination.

We believe that in Africa the bourgeoisie still has a role

to play today. This is quite different from Latin America where the national bourgeoisie no longer has any choice but to submit completely to the tutelage of imperialism. In many independent African countries, the bourgeoisie has, in the beginning, the possibility of developing and of playing a relatively progressive role. It can, for a time, mobilize the people and the forces of the left around them under the slogan of the struggle against imperialism, but inevitably the moment comes when the bourgeoisie, and the government representing it, end up at a dead end. It is not possible for the bourgeoisie, by its very nature, to follow the road onto which the people seek to push it. The only course remaining open to it is collaboration with imperialism and oppression of the people. In brief, it can be said that there are at present great possibilities in Africa because of the upsurge in this region of the world but that there are also real dangers that we have to keep in mind. There are important economic problems that must be remembered. Unequal relations in international trade lead to an impasse where it becomes very easy to concede to imperialism and to oppress the people whom, for a short period, they appear to serve.

JOSIE FANON: If you were asked what road of economic development was best suited for the African countries, what would be your response?

CHE GUEVARA: If my advice were asked, or rather my opinion, as Cuban minister of industry, I would say simply that a country beginning to develop itself must, in the first period, work, above all at organization, and that one should approach the practical problems thinking with one's own head. This may seem to be an abstract and rather vague opinion but it's something very important.

In Africa, where many countries have already carried out very extensive nationalizations, there is perhaps the possibility of creating certain enterprises to provide products for other countries lacking them and vice versa. It is necessary to work in the spirit of mutual interest and for that it is necessary to know each other better and to establish relations of trust. At first this must be limited to very simple things. It may be necessary at times to set up small factories requiring a lot of labor power that will enable many unemployed to get jobs, rather than highly mechanized enterprises employing only a few workers. In certain cases, a sector must be rapidly mechanized; in other cases this is not necessary. In fact, in a country on the road to development most problems involve agriculture and extractive industry. It is quite evident, however, that these problems are posed in a different way in each country, and that one must pay attention above all to particular realities. That's why it is impossible to give a general formula that could be applied to all African countries.

JOSIE FANON: What are the perspectives in your opinion for the revolutionary struggle in Latin America?

CHE GUEVARA: You are aware that this is something that particularly interests me; it's my deepest desire. We believe that the revolutionary struggle is a very long and a very hard struggle. It is extremely difficult to believe—difficult, but clearly not impossible—in the isolated triumph of the revolution in one country. Imperialism has been preparing an organized repression of the peoples of Latin America for some years. In different countries they have formed an International of repression. Right now, in fact, in the Latin American country where the last battles were fought for the liberation of Latin America from the Spanish yoke, in Peru, military maneuvers are being held. Various countries are participating in these maneuvers, led by the United States, in the Ayacucho region. What we are witnessing in this region is direct preparations for repression. And why are these maneuvers taking place precisely in this mountainous region of Peru, in this jungle zone? It is simply because Ayacucho is situated close to the place where important revolutionary bases exist. Ayacucho was not chosen by accident.

The North Americans are paying a lot of attention to the problem of guerrilla warfare. They have written some very interesting things on this. They have grasped the quite correct idea that guerrilla warfare is extremely difficult to eliminate unless this is done in its very early stages. All their strategy is now oriented toward this objective, taking two main forms: first of all, repression; secondly, the isolation of the revolutionists from their main base—the peasants. I have read in a U.S. document the very expression used by Mao Tse-tung: *Among the people, revolutionists are like a fish in water.* The North Americans have grasped that the power of the guerrilla force resides in this, and they have grasped that everything must be done to stop this from continuing.

Clearly, all these factors will make the struggle more difficult. But against the International of repression will come the inevitable and natural reply of the International of struggle of the proletarians and peasants against the common enemy. That is why we foresee the organization of a continental front of struggle against imperialism and its domestic allies. This front will take a long time to organize, but when it materializes it will be a severe blow against imperialism. I don't know if it will be a definitive blow, but it will be a very strong one. It is for this reason that we pose this fundamental principle: The struggle for liberation must be not only a defensive struggle, but likewise an offensive struggle against imperialism.

We will add that the working class in the United States, because of its high standard of living, does not clearly see the contradictions existing in U.S. society. To the U.S. working class, these contradictions, which are blunted, appear incomprehensible and they cannot gain clear consciousness of their own exploitation as long as they continue to get the crumbs that U.S. imperialism tosses to them from the feast.

At the Afro-Asian conference

From Algeria Guevara traveled to Mali, Congo (Brazzaville), Guinea, Ghana, Dahomey, Tanzania, and the United Arab Republic. He then returned to Algiers to attend the Second Economic Seminar of the Organization of Afro-Asian Solidarity. The speech he made there, particularly in its passages regarding economic relations between underdeveloped countries and the countries of the Soviet bloc, was one of the most important of his career. His speech, delivered on February 24, 1965, is here translated in full.

Dear brothers:

Cuba is here at this conference to speak on behalf of the peoples of Latin America. As we have emphasized on other occasions, Cuba also speaks as an underdeveloped country as well as one that is building socialism.

It is not by accident that our delegation is permitted to give its opinion here, in the circle of the peoples of Asia and Africa. A common aspiration unites us in our march toward the future: the defeat of imperialism. A common past of struggle against the same enemy has united us along the road.

This is an assembly of peoples in struggle, and the struggle is developing on two equally important fronts that require all our efforts. The struggle against imperialism, for liberation from colonial or neocolonial shackles, which is being carried out by means of political weapons, firearms, or a combination of the two, is not separate from the struggle against backwardness and poverty. Both are stages on the same road leading toward the creation of a new society of justice and plenty.

It is imperative to take political power and get rid of the oppressor classes. But then the second stage of the struggle, which may be even more difficult than the first, must be faced.

Ever since monopoly capital took over the world, it has kept the greater part of humanity in poverty, dividing all the profits among the group of the most powerful countries. The standard of living in those countries is based on the extreme poverty of our countries. To raise the living standards of the underdeveloped nations, therefore, we must fight against imperialism. And each time a country is torn away from the imperialist tree, it is not only a partial battle won against the main enemy, but it also contributes to the real weakening of that enemy and is one step more toward the final victory.

There are no borders in this struggle to the death. We cannot be indifferent to what happens anywhere in the world, because a victory by any country over imperialism is our victory, just as any country's defeat is a defeat for all of us. The practice of proletarian internationalism is not only a duty for the peoples struggling for a better future, it is also an inescapable necessity. If the imperialist enemy, the United States or any other, carries out its attack against the underdeveloped peoples and the socialist countries, elementary logic determines the need for an alliance between the underdeveloped peoples and the socialist countries. If there were no other uniting factor, the common enemy should be it.

Of course these alliances cannot be made spontaneously, without discussions, without birth pangs, which sometimes can be painful.

Each time a country is liberated, we said, it is a defeat for the world imperialist system. But we must agree that the break is not achieved by the mere act of proclaiming independence or winning an armed victory in a revolution. It is achieved when imperialist economic domination over a people is brought to an end. Therefore, it is a matter of vital interest to the socialist countries for a real break to take place. And it is our international duty, a duty determined by our guiding ideology, to contribute our efforts to make this liberation as rapid and deep-going as possible.

A conclusion must be drawn from all this: the socialist countries must help pay for the development of countries now starting out on the road to liberation. We state it this way with no intention whatsoever of blackmail or theatrics, nor are we looking for an easy way to get closer to the Afro-Asian peoples; it is our profound conviction. Socialism cannot exist without a change in consciousness resulting in a new fraternal attitude toward humanity, both at an individual level, within the societies where socialism is being built or has been built, and on a world scale, with regard to all peoples suffering from imperialist oppression.

We believe the responsibility of aiding dependent countries must be approached in such a spirit. There should not be any more talk about developing mutually beneficial trade based on prices forced on the backward countries by the law of value and the international relations of unequal exchange that result from the law of value.

How can it be "mutually beneficial" to sell at world market prices the raw materials that cost the underdeveloped countries immeasurable sweat and suffering, and to buy at world market prices the machinery produced in today's big automated factories?

If we establish that kind of relation between the two groups of nations, we must agree that the socialist countries are, in a certain way, accomplices of imperial exploitation. It can be argued that the amount of exchange with the underdeveloped countries is an insignificant part of the foreign trade of the socialist countries. That is very true, but it does not eliminate the immoral character of the exchange.

The socialist countries have the moral duty to put an end to their tacit complicity with the exploiting countries of the West. The fact that the trade today is small means nothing. In 1959 Cuba only occasionally sold sugar to some socialist bloc country, usually through English brokers or brokers of other nationalities. And today, 80 percent of Cuba's trade is with that area. All its vital supplies come from the socialist camp, and in fact it has joined that camp. We cannot say that this entrance into the socialist camp was brought about merely by the increase in trade. Nor was the increase in trade brought about by the destruction of the old structures and the adoption of the socialist form of development. Both sides of the question intersect and are interrelated.

We did not start out on the road that ends in communism foreseeing all steps as logically predetermined by an ideology advancing toward a fixed goal. The truths of socialism plus the raw truths of imperialism forged our people and showed them the path that we have now taken consciously. To advance toward their own complete liberation, the peoples of Asia and Africa must take the same path. They will follow it sooner or later, regardless of what modifying adjective their socialism may take today.

For us there is no valid definition of socialism other than abolition of the exploitation of man by man. As long as this has not been achieved, if we think we are in the stage of building socialism but instead of ending exploitation the work of suppressing it comes to a halt, or worse, is reversed—then we cannot even speak of building socialism.

We have to prepare conditions so that our brothers can directly and consciously take the path of the complete abolition of exploitation, but we cannot ask them to take that path if we ourselves are accomplices in that exploitation. If we were asked what methods are used to establish fair prices, we could not answer because we do not know the full scope of the practical problems involved. All we know is that, after political discussions, the Soviet Union and Cuba have signed agreements advantageous to us, by means of which we will sell five million tons of sugar at prices set above those of the so-called free world sugar market. The People's Republic of China also pays those prices in buying from us.

This is only a beginning. The real task consists of setting prices that will permit development. A great change of ideas will be involved in changing the order of international relations. Foreign trade should not determine policy, but should on the contrary be subordinated to a fraternal policy toward the peoples.

Let us briefly analyze the problem of long-term credits for developing basic industries. Frequently we find that beneficiary countries attempt to establish an industrial base disproportionate to their present capacity. The products will not be consumed domestically and the country's reserves will be risked in the undertaking.

Our thinking is as follows: The investments of the socialist states in their own territory come directly out of the state budget, and are recovered only by the use of the products throughout the entire manufacturing process, down to the finished goods. We propose that some thought be given to the possibility of making these kinds of investments in the underdeveloped countries. In this way we could unleash an immense force, hidden in our continents, which have been exploited miserably but never aided in their development.

We could begin a new stage of a real international division of labor, based not on the history of what has been done up to now, but rather on the future history of what can be done.

The states in whose territories the new investments are to be made would have all the inherent rights of sovereign property over them with no payment or credits involved. But they would be obligated to supply agreed-upon quantities of products to the investor countries for a certain number of years at set prices.

The method for financing the local portion of expenses incurred by a country receiving investments of this kind also deserves study. The supply of marketable goods on long-term credits to the governments of underdeveloped countries could be one form of aid not requiring the contribution of freely convertible hard currency.

Another difficult problem that must be solved is the mastering of technology. The shortage of technicians in underdeveloped countries is well known to us all. Educational institutions and teachers are lacking. Sometimes we lack a real understanding of our needs and have not made the decision to carry out a top-priority policy of technical, cultural, and ideological development.

The socialist countries should supply the aid to organize institutions for technical education. They should insist on the great importance of this and should supply technical cadres to fill the present need.

It is necessary to further emphasize this last point. The technicians who come to our countries must be exemplary. They are comrades who will face a strange environment, often one hostile to technology, with a different language and totally different customs. The technicians who take on this difficult task must be, first of all, communists in the most profound and noble sense of the word. With this single quality, plus a modicum of flexibility and organization, wonders can be achieved.

We know this can be done. Because fraternal countries have sent us a certain number of technicians who have done more for the development of our country than ten institutes, and have contributed more to our friendship than ten ambassadors or a hundred diplomatic receptions.

If we could achieve the above-listed points—and if all the technology of the advanced countries could be placed within reach of the underdeveloped countries, unhampered by the present system of patents, which prevents the spread of inventions of different countries—we would progress a great deal in our common task.

Imperialism has been defeated in many partial battles. But it remains a considerable force in the world. We cannot expect its final defeat save through effort and sacrifice on the part of us all.

The proposed set of measures, however, cannot be implemented unilaterally. The socialist countries should help pay for the development of the underdeveloped countries, we agree. But the underdeveloped countries must also steel their forces to embark resolutely on the road of building a new society—whatever name one gives it—where the machine, an instrument of labor, is no longer an instrument for the exploitation of man by man. Nor can the confidence of the socialist countries be expected by those who play at balancing between capitalism and socialism, trying to use each force as a counterweight in order to derive certain advantages from such competition. A new policy of absolute seriousness should govern the relations between the two groups of societies. It is worth emphasizing once again that the means of production should preferably be in the hands of the state, so that the marks of exploitation may gradually disappear.

Furthermore, development cannot be left to complete improvisation. It is necessary to plan the construction of the new society. Planning is one of the laws of socialism, and without it, socialism would not exist. Without correct planning there can be no adequate guarantee that all the various sectors of a country's economy will combine harmoniously to take the leaps forward that our epoch demands.

Planning cannot be left as an isolated problem of each of our small countries, distorted in their development, possessors of some raw materials or producers of some manufactured or semimanufactured goods, but lacking in most others. From the outset, planning should take on a certain regional dimension in order to intermix the various national economies, and thus bring about an integration on a basis that is truly mutually beneficial.

We believe the road ahead is full of dangers, not dangers conjured up or foreseen in the distant future by some superior mind, but palpable dangers deriving from the realities besetting us. The fight against colonialism has reached its final stages, but in the present era colonial status is only a consequence of imperialist domination. As long as imperialism exists it will, by definition, exert its domination over other countries. Today that domination is called neocolonialism.

Neocolonialism developed first in South America, throughout a whole continent, and today it begins to be felt with increasing intensity in Africa and Asia. Its forms of penetration and development have different characteristics. One is the brutal form we have seen in the Congo. Brute force, without any respect or concealment whatsoever, is its extreme weapon. There is another, more subtle form: penetration into countries that win political independence, linking up with the nascent local bourgeoisies, development of a parasitic bourgeois class closely allied to the metropolitan interests. This development is based on a certain temporary rise in the people's standard of living, because in a very backward country the simple step from feudal to capitalist relations marks a big advance, regardless of the dire consequences for the workers in the long run.

Neocolonialism has bared its claws in the Congo. That is not a sign of strength, but of weakness. It had to resort to force, its extreme weapon, as an economic argument. This has generated very intense opposing reactions. But at the same time, a much more subtle form of neocolonialism is being practiced in other countries of Africa and Asia. It is rapidly bringing about what some have called the South Americanization of these continents; that is, the development of a parasitic bourgeoisie that adds nothing to the national wealth of their countries, but rather deposits its huge ill-gotten profits in capitalist banks abroad, and makes deals with foreign countries to reap more profits with absolute disregard for the welfare of the people.

There are also other dangers, such as competition between fraternal countries that are politically friendly and sometimes neighbors, as both try to develop the same investments simultaneously to produce for markets that often cannot absorb the increased volume. This competition has the disadvantage of wasting energies that could be used to achieve much greater economic coordination; furthermore, it gives the imperialist monopolies room to maneuver.

When it has been impossible to carry out a given investment project with the aid of the socialist camp, there have been occasions when it has been carried out by signing agreements with the capitalists. Such capitalist investments have the disadvantage not only of the terms of the loans, but other, much more important disadvantages as well, such as establishment of joint ventures with a dangerous neighbor. Since these investments in general parallel those made in other states, they tend to cause divisions between friendly countries by creating economic rivalries. Furthermore, they create the dangers of corruption flowing from the constant presence of capitalism, which is very skillful in conjuring up visions of advancement and well-being to fog the minds of many people.

Sometime later, prices drop in the market saturated by similar products. The affected countries are obliged to seek new loans, or to permit additional investments in order to compete. The final consequences of such a policy are the fall of the economy into the hands of the monopolies, and a slow but sure return to the past. As we see it, the only safe method for investments is direct participation by the state as the sole purchaser of the goods, limiting imperialist activity to contracts for supplies and not letting them set one foot inside our house. And here it is just and proper to take advantage of interimperialist contradictions in order to secure the least burdensome terms.

We have to watch out for "disinterested" economic, cultural, and other aid that imperialism grants directly or through puppet states, which gets a better reception in some parts of the world.

If all of these dangers are not seen in time, some countries that began their task of national liberation with faith and enthusiasm may find themselves on the neocolonial road, as monopoly domination is subtly established step by step so that its effects are difficult to discern until they brutally make themselves felt.

There is a big job to be done. Immense problems confront our two worlds—that of the socialist countries and that called the Third World—problems directly concerning man and his welfare, and related to the struggle against the main force that bears the responsibility for our backwardness. In the face of these problems, all countries and peoples conscious of their duties, of the dangers involved in the situation, of the sacrifices required by development, must take concrete steps to cement our friendship in the two fields that can never be separated, the economic and the political. And we should organize a great solid bloc that, in its turn, helps new countries to free themselves not only from the political power of imperialism but also from its economic power.

The question of liberation by armed struggle from an oppressor political power should be dealt with in accordance with the rules of proletarian internationalism. In a socialist country at war, it would be absurd to conceive of a factory manager demanding guaranteed payment before shipping to the front the tanks produced by his factory. It ought to seem no less absurd to inquire of a people fighting for liberation, or needing arms to defend its freedom, whether or not they can guarantee payment.

Arms cannot be commodities in our world. They must be delivered to the peoples asking for them to use against the common enemy, with no charge and in the quantities needed and available. That is the spirit in which the USSR and the People's Republic of China have offered us their military aid. We are socialists; we constitute a guarantee of the proper utilization of those arms. But we are not the only ones, and all of us should receive the same treatment.

The reply to the ominous attacks by United States imperialism against Vietnam or the Congo should be to supply those sister countries with all the defense equipment they need, and to offer them our full solidarity without any conditions whatsoever.

In the economic field we must conquer the road to development with the most advanced technology possible. We cannot set out to follow the long ascending steps from feudalism to the nuclear and automated era. That would be a road of immense and largely useless sacrifices. We have to start from technology at its current level. We have to make the great technological leap forward that will reduce the current gap between the more developed countries and ourselves. Technology must be applied to the large factories and also to a properly developed agriculture. Above all, its foundation must be technological and ideological education, with a sufficient mass base and strength to sustain the research institutes and organizations that have to be created in each country, as well as the men who will use the existing technology and be capable of adapting themselves to the newly mastered technology.

These cadres must have a clear awareness of their duty to the society in which they live. There cannot be adequate technological education if it is not complemented by ideological education—nor without that, in most of our countries, can there be an adequate foundation for industrial development, which is what determines the development of a modern society, nor the most basic consumer goods and adequate schooling.

A good part of the national revenues must be spent on so-called unproductive investment in education. And priority must be given to the development of agricultural productivity. The latter has reached truly incredible levels in many capitalist countries, producing the senseless crisis of overproduction and a surplus of grain and other food products or industrial raw materials in the developed countries. While the rest of the world goes hungry, these countries have enough land and labor to produce several times over what is needed to feed the entire world.

Agriculture must be considered a fundamental pillar of our development. Therefore, a fundamental aspect of our work should be changes in the agrarian structure, and adaptation to the new technological possibilities and to the new obligations of eliminating the exploitation of man.

Before making costly decisions that could cause irreparable damage, a careful survey of the national territory is needed. This is one of the preliminary steps in economic research and a basic prerequisite for correct planning.

We warmly support Algeria's proposal for institutionalizing our relations. We would just like to make some supplementary suggestions:

First: in order for the union to be an instrument in the struggle against imperialism, the cooperation of Latin

American countries and an alliance with the socialist countries is necessary.

Second: we should be vigilant to preserve the revolutionary character of the union, preventing the admission into it of governments or movements not identified with the general aspirations of the people, and creating mechanisms that would permit the separation from it of any government or popular movement diverging from the just road.

Third: we must advocate the establishment of new relations on an equal footing between our countries and the capitalist ones, creating a revolutionary jurisprudence to defend ourselves in case of conflict, and to give new meaning to the relations between ourselves and the rest of the world.

We speak a revolutionary language and we honestly fight for the victory of that cause. But frequently we entangle ourselves in the nets of an international law created as the result of confrontations between the imperialist powers, and not by the free peoples, the just peoples, in the course of their struggles.

For example, our peoples suffer the painful pressure of foreign bases established on their territories, or they have to carry the heavy burdens of foreign debts of incredible size. The story of these throwbacks is well known to all of us. Puppet governments, governments weakened by long struggles for liberation or the operation of the laws of the capitalist market, have allowed treaties that threaten our internal stability and jeopardize our future. Now is the time to throw off the yoke, to force renegotiation of oppressive foreign debts, and to force the imperialists to abandon their bases of aggression.

I would not want to conclude these remarks, this recitation of concepts you all know, without calling the attention of this gathering to the fact that Cuba is not the only Latin American country; it is simply the only one that has the opportunity of speaking before you today. Other peoples are shedding their blood to win the rights we have. When we send our greetings from here, and from all the conferences and the places where they may be held, to the heroic peoples of Vietnam, Laos, so-called Portuguese Guinea, South Africa, or Palestine—to all exploited countries fighting for their emancipation—we must simultaneously extend our voice of friendship, our hand, and our encouragement, to our brother peoples in Venezuela, Guatemala, and Colombia, who today, arms in hand, are resolutely saying "No!" to the imperialist enemy.

Few settings from which to make this declaration are as symbolic as Algiers, one of the most heroic capitals of freedom. May the magnificent Algerian people—schooled as few others in sufferings for independence, under the decisive leadership of its party, headed by our dear compañero Ahmed Ben Bella—serve as an inspiration to us in this fight without quarter against world imperialism.

Interview with 'Libération'

On March 14, 1965, Guevara left Algeria to return to Cuba. Before leaving, he granted the following interview to Boualam Rouissi of the Casablanca, Morocco, weekly *Libération*. It appeared in the March 17–23 issue of that periodical.

QUESTION: Mr. Minister, since this is the first time that Cuba has participated as a full member in a conference of the Afro-Asian Organization, I would like to ask you first how you visualize widening this organization to include Latin America?

ANSWER: I think that the Organization of Afro-Asian Solidarity can be widened to include Latin America quite easily. The procedural question is not of any importance. The real problem resides in the fact that in Latin America there is hardly a government that is struggling against imperialism. It is necessary to designate popular movements. But there are more movements that call themselves popular than really live up to the name. In any case, the Secretariat of the Organization of Afro-Asian Solidarity has been able to work out some concrete proposals on this point.

QUESTION: You have just made a tour of Africa; could you tell us about the aim of your trip as well as your impressions of the general situation in Africa in relation to the needs of the struggle against neocolonialism?

ANSWER: The aim of the tour I just made of Africa was to strengthen the ties between Cuba and the African countries. It enabled me to explain the Cuban revolution and particularly to learn.

I think that the struggle against neocolonialism is one form of the struggle against imperialism. The struggle against neocolonialism and the struggle against imperialism can be separated for tactical reasons, but it must be kept in mind that it's the same struggle against the same enemy. Despite their own differences, the imperialists under the leadership of the U.S.A. are united in the Congo and wherever there is a confrontation over an issue of importance for the future of Africa. That's why the struggle against such neocolonialist countries cannot be separated from the general struggle against imperialism.

There is an alternative that appears approximately as follows:

Either the progressive countries constitute a homogenous bloc in order to struggle against U.S. imperialism in the Congo, and after the victory against imperialism there, continue the struggle against the neocolonialist countries that constitute the bases of aggression (naturally, this is not a question of a military struggle).

Or the situation will remain fluid, permitting the Americans to strike separate blows at the weakest countries (it is necessary to draw the lesson of the assassination of the prime minister of Burundi and what followed). In this case the progressive countries will be partially isolated at the moment when they should struggle against the American penetration, beginning in the Congo.

In short, the battle of the Congo must, for the African countries, have the meaning of a historic stage that will either determine their advance or their retreat. Victory in the Congo will show the Africans that national liberation opens the way for the construction of socialism; a defeat will open the way for neocolonialism. Socialism or neocolonialism, that is the stake for all of Africa in the encounter now taking place in the Congo.

QUESTION: Many African countries are still under imperialist domination reminiscent of Cuba under Batista. I would like to ask you to tell us what the characteristic elements of the situation were in Cuba that brought about the revolution.

ANSWER: The situation in Cuba under Batista was not much different from that of the African countries you mention. In particular, Cuba was a neocolonialized country where the national bourgeoisie had played out its role. In this sense, Cuba was already "ripe" for the revolution. But in another sense, the situation in Cuba was not any "riper" objectively than other places in Latin America; it could even be said that it was more advanced in Guatemala or Argentina.

But what is most important is not the "objective conditions" but the subjective conditions; that is, in the final analysis, the determination of the revolutionary movement. The revolution is not an apple that falls when it is ripe! You have to make it fall, and it was precisely this that was our historic role, especially Fidel Castro's.

QUESTION: The Cuban revolution has sometimes been considered to be an "exceptional phenomenon."

ANSWER: There was one exceptional phenomenon in my opinion, that was the presence of a man who, against the dogmatic conceptions, against the "waiting" or defeatist attitudes that dominated the revolutionary forces, was able to see farther, to show the people the road, and stay at the head of the revolution during the armed struggle and today during the construction of socialism. I don't know if it's necessary to name him!

But the problem remains posed. Is a Fidel Castro indispensable to a revolution?

Within the framework of the Cuban revolution, perhaps Fidel Castro was necessary to show the road, to demonstrate that it was possible to do what he did with his people. But if Fidel Castro was necessary to our revolution, more Fidels are not necessary for other revolutions!

Yesterday the progressive movement was hunting with a magnifying glass for the exact moment when the "objective conditions" and the subjective conditions would coincide and provoke the revolution, without, however, ever finding it!

Today, the danger is different—to start hunting with the same magnifying glass for a Fidel Castro!

And what is lost in the second case is not something small, but political power, which must be the first task of the revolutionist. Until he has obtained it, he has done nothing.

Socialism and man in Cuba

Guevara wrote "Notes for the Study of Socialism and Man in Cuba" in the form of a letter to Carlos Quijano, editor of *Marcha,* an independent radical weekly published in Montevideo, Uruguay. It bore the dateline "Havana, 1965." In addition to appearing in *Marcha,* it was printed by *Verde Olivo,* the magazine of the Cuban armed forces. It is translated in full below.

Dear compañero:

Though belatedly, I am completing these notes in the course of my trip through Africa, hoping in this way to keep my promise. I would like to do so by dealing with the theme set forth in the title above. I think it may be of interest to Uruguayan readers.

A common argument from the mouths of capitalist spokesmen, in the ideological struggle against socialism, is that socialism, or the period of building socialism into which we have entered, is characterized by the abolition of the individual for the sake of the state. I will not try to refute this argument solely on theoretical grounds, but rather to establish the facts as they exist in Cuba and then add comments of a general nature. Let me begin by broadly sketching the history of our revolutionary struggle before and after the taking of power.

As is well known, the exact date of the beginning of the revolutionary struggle—which would culminate in January 1959—was July 26, 1953. A group of men led by Fidel Castro attacked the Moncada garrison in Oriente province on the morning of that day. The attack was a failure; the failure became a disaster; and the survivors ended up in prison, beginning the revolutionary struggle again after they were freed by an amnesty.

In this process, in which there was only the germ of socialism, man was a fundamental factor. We put our trust in him—individual, specific, with a first and last name—and the triumph or failure of the mission entrusted to him depended on his capacity for action.

Then came the stage of guerrilla struggle. It developed in two distinct environments: the people, the still sleeping mass that had to be mobilized; and its vanguard, the guerrillas, the motor force of the mobilization, the generator of revolutionary consciousness and militant enthusiasm. This vanguard was the catalyzing agent that created the subjective conditions necessary for victory.

Here again, in the framework of the proletarianization of our thinking, of this revolution that took place in our habits and our minds, the individual was the basic factor. Every one of the fighters of the Sierra Maestra who reached an upper rank in the revolutionary forces has a record of outstanding deeds to his credit. They attained their rank on this basis. It was the first heroic period, and in it they competed for the heaviest responsibilities, for the greatest dangers, with no other satisfaction than fulfilling a duty.

In our work of revolutionary education we frequently return to this instructive theme. In the attitude of our fighters could be glimpsed the man of the future.

On other occasions in our history the act of total dedication to the revolutionary cause was repeated. During the October [1962 missile] crisis and in the days of Hurricane Flora we saw exceptional deeds of valor and sacrifice performed by an entire people. Finding the method to perpetuate this heroic attitude in daily life is, from the ideological standpoint, one of our fundamental tasks.

In January 1959 the revolutionary government was established with the participation of various members of the treacherous bourgeoisie. The presence of the Rebel Army as the basic element of strength constituted the guarantee of power.

Serious contradictions developed right away. In the first instance, in February 1959, these were resolved when Fidel Castro assumed leadership of the government, taking the post of prime minister. This process culminated in July of the same year with the resignation under mass pressure of President Urrutia.

In the history of the Cuban revolution there now appeared a character, well-defined in its features, who would systematically reappear: the mass.

This multifaceted being is not, as is claimed, the sum of elements of the same type (reduced, moreover, to that same type by the reigning system), which acts like a flock of sheep. It is true that it follows its leaders, basically Fidel Castro, without hesitation. But the degree to which he won this trust results precisely from having interpreted the people's desires and aspirations in their full meaning, and from the sincere struggle to fulfill the promises he made.

The mass participated in the agrarian reform and in the difficult task of the administration of state enterprises; it went through the heroic experience of Playa Girón; it was hardened in the battles against various bands of bandits armed by the CIA; it lived through one of the most important decisions of modern times during the October crisis; and today it continues to work for the building of socialism.

Viewed superficially, it might appear that those who speak of the subordination of the individual to the state are right. The mass carries out with matchless enthusiasm and discipline the tasks set by the government, whether in the field of the economy, culture, defense, sports, etc.

The initiative generally comes from Fidel or from the revolutionary high command and is explained to the people, who make it their own. In some cases the party and government take a local experience and generalize it, following the same procedure.

Nevertheless, the state sometimes makes mistakes. When one of these mistakes occurs, one notes a decline in collective enthusiasm due to the effect of a quantitative decrease in each of the elements that make up the mass. Work is paralyzed until it is reduced to insignificant amounts. It is time to make a correction. That is what happened in March 1962, as a result of the sectarian policy imposed on the party by Aníbal Escalante.

Clearly this mechanism is not enough to ensure a succession of sensible measures. A more structured connection with the mass is needed, and we must improve it in the course of the next years. But as far as initiatives originating in the upper strata of the government are concerned, we are currently utilizing the almost intuitive method of sounding out general reactions to the great problems we confront.

In this Fidel is a master. His own special way of fusing himself with the people can be appreciated only by seeing him in action. At the great public mass meetings one can observe something like the dialogue of two tuning forks whose vibrations interact, producing new sounds. Fidel and the mass begin to vibrate together in a dialogue of growing intensity until they reach the climax in an abrupt conclusion crowned by our cry of struggle and victory.

The difficult thing to understand for someone not living through the experience of the revolution is this close dialectical unity between the individual and the mass in which both are interrelated and, at the same time, in which the mass, as an aggregate of individuals, interacts with its leaders.

Some phenomena of this kind can be seen under capitalism, when politicians appear who are capable of mobilizing popular opinion. But when these are not genuine social movements—if they were, it would not be entirely correct to call them capitalist—they live only so long as the individual who inspires them, or until the harshness of capitalist society puts an end to the people's illusions.

In capitalist society man is controlled by a pitiless law usually beyond his comprehension. The alienated human specimen is tied to society as a whole by an invisible umbilical cord: the law of value. This law acts upon all aspects of his life, shaping his course and destiny.

The laws of capitalism, which are blind and are invisible to ordinary people, act upon the individual without his being aware of it. He sees only the vastness of a seemingly infinite horizon before him. That is how it is painted by capitalist propagandists who purport to draw a lesson from the example of Rockefeller—whether or not it is true—about the possibilities of success. The amount of poverty and suffering required for a Rockefeller to emerge, and the amount of depravity entailed in the accumulation of a fortune of such magnitude, are left out of the picture, and it is not always possible for the popular forces to make these concepts clear.

(A discussion of how the workers in the imperialist countries gradually lose the spirit of working-class internationalism due to a certain degree of complicity in the exploitation of the dependent countries, and how this at the same time weakens the combativity of the masses in the imperialist countries, would be appropriate here, but that is a theme which goes beyond the aim of these notes.)

In any case the road to success is pictured as beset with perils—perils that, it would seem, an individual with the proper qualities can overcome to attain the goal. The reward is seen in the distance; the way is lonely. Furthermore, it is a contest among wolves. Onc can win only at the cost of the failure of others.

I would now like to try to define the individual, the actor in this strange and moving drama of the building of socialism, in his dual existence as a unique being and as a member of society.

I think the place to start is to recognize his quality of incompleteness, of being an unfinished product. The vestiges of the past are brought into the present in the individual consciousness, and a continual labor is necessary to eradicate them. The process is two-sided. On the one side, society acts through direct and indirect education; on the other, the individual submits himself to a conscious process of self-education.

The new society in formation has to compete fiercely with the past. This past makes itself felt not only in the individual consciousness—in which the residue of an education systematically oriented toward isolating the individual still weighs heavily—but also through the very character of this transition period in which commodity relations still persist. The commodity is the economic cell of capitalist society. So long as it exists its effects will make themselves felt in the organization of production and, consequently, in consciousness.

Marx outlined the transition period as resulting from the explosive transformation of the capitalist system destroyed by its own contradictions. In historical reality, however, we have seen that some countries that were weak limbs on the tree of imperialism were torn off first—a phenomenon foreseen by Lenin.

In these countries capitalism had developed sufficiently to make its effects felt by the people in one way or another. But it was not capitalism's internal contradictions that, having exhausted all possibilities, caused the system to explode. The struggle for liberation from a foreign oppressor; the misery caused by external events such as war, whose consequences privileged classes place on the backs of the exploited; liberation movements aimed at overthrowing neocolonial regimes—these are the usual factors in unleashing this kind of explosion. Conscious action does the rest.

A complete education for social labor has not yet taken place in these countries, and wealth is far from being within the reach of the masses through the simple process of appropriation. Underdevelopment, on the one hand, and the usual flight of capital to the "civilized" countries, on the other, make a rapid transition without sacrifices impossible. There remains a long way to go in constructing the economic base, and the temptation is very great to follow the beaten track of material interest as the lever with which to accelerate development.

There is the danger that the forest will not be seen for the trees. The pipe dream that socialism can be achieved with the help of the dull instruments left to us by capitalism (the commodity as the economic cell, profitability, individual material interest as a lever, etc.) can lead into a blind alley. And you wind up there after having traveled a long distance with many crossroads, and it is hard to figure out just where you took the wrong turn. Meanwhile, the economic foundation that has been laid has done its work of undermining the development of consciousness. To build communism it is necessary, simultaneous with the new material foundations, to build the new man.

That is why it is very important to choose the right instrument for mobilizing the masses. Basically, this instrument must be moral in character, without neglecting, however, a correct use of the material incentive—especially of a social character.

As I have already said, in moments of great peril it is easy to muster a powerful response to moral incentives. Retaining their effect, however, requires the development of a consciousness in which there is a new scale of values. Society as a whole must be converted into a gigantic school.

In rough outline this phenomenon is similar to the process by which capitalist consciousness was formed in its initial period. Capitalism uses force but it also educates people in the system. Direct propaganda is carried out by those entrusted with explaining the inevitability of class society, either through some theory of divine origin or a mechanical theory of natural law. This lulls the masses, since they see themselves as being oppressed by an evil against which it is impossible to struggle.

Next comes hope of improvement—and in this, capitalism differed from the earlier caste systems, which offered no way out. For some people, the principle of the caste system will remain in effect: The reward for the obedient is to be transported after death to some fabulous other world where, according to the old beliefs, good people are rewarded. For other people there is this innovation: class divisions are determined by fate, but individuals can rise out of their class through work, initiative, etc. This process, and the myth of the self-made man, are profoundly hypocritical: it is the self-serving effort to turn a lie into the truth.

In our case direct education acquires a much greater importance. The explanation is convincing because it is true; no subterfuge is needed. It is carried on by the state's educational apparatus as a function of general, technical, and ideological education through such agencies as the Ministry of Education and the party's informational apparatus. Education takes hold among the masses and the foreseen new attitude tends to become a habit. The masses continue to make it their own and to influence those who have not yet educated themselves. This is the indirect form of educating the masses, as powerful as the other.

But the process is a conscious one. The individual continually feels the impact of the new social power and perceives that he does not entirely measure up to its standards. Under the pressure of indirect education, he tries to adjust himself to a situation that he feels is right and that his own lack of development had prevented him from reaching previously. He educates himself.

In this period of the building of socialism we can see the new man being born. His image is not yet completely finished—it never will be, since the process goes forward hand in hand with the development of new economic forms.

Aside from those whose lack of education makes them take the solitary road toward satisfying their own personal ambitions, there are those—even within this new panorama of a unified march forward—who have a tendency to walk separate from the masses accompanying them. What is important, however, is that each day men are acquiring ever more consciousness of the need for their incorporation into society and, at the same time, of their importance as the motor of that society.

They no longer travel completely alone over lost roads toward distant aspirations. They follow their vanguard, consisting of the party, the advanced workers, the advanced men who walk in unity with the masses and in close communion with them. The vanguards have their eyes fixed on the future and its reward, but it is not a vision of something for the individual. The prize is the new society in which men will have different characteristics: the society of communist man.

The road is long and full of difficulties. At times we lose our way and must turn back. At other times we go too fast and separate ourselves from the masses. Sometimes we go too slow and feel the hot breath of those treading at our heels. In our zeal as revolutionists we try to move ahead as fast as possible, clearing the way. But we know we must draw our nourishment from the mass and that it can advance more rapidly only if we inspire it by our example.

Despite the importance given to moral incentives, the fact that there remains a division into two main groups (excluding, of course, the minority that for one reason or another does not participate in the building of socialism) indicates the relative lack of development of social consciousness. The vanguard group is ideologically more advanced than the mass; the latter understands the new values, but not sufficiently. While among the former there has been a qualitative change that enables them to make sacrifices in their capacity as an advance guard, the latter see only part of the picture and must be subject to incentives and pressures of a certain intensity. This is the dictatorship of the proletariat operating not only on the defeated class but also on individuals of the victorious class.

All of this means that for total success a series of mechanisms, of revolutionary institutions, is needed. Along with the image of the multitudes marching toward the future comes the concept of institutionalization as a harmonious set of channels, steps, restraints, and well-oiled mechanisms that facilitate the advance, that facilitate the natural selection of those destined to march in the vanguard, and that bestow rewards on those who fulfill their duties and punishments on those who commit a crime against the society that is being built.

This institutionalization of the revolution has not yet been achieved. We are looking for something new that will permit a complete identification between the government and the community in its entirety, something appropriate to the special conditions of the building of socialism, while avoiding to the utmost a transplanting of the commonplaces of bourgeois democracy—such as legislative chambers, for example—into the society in formation.

Some experiments aimed at the gradual institutionalization of the revolution have been made, but without undue haste. The greatest brake has been our fear lest any appearance of formality might separate us from the masses and from the individual, might make us lose sight of the ultimate and most important revolutionary aspiration: to see man liberated from his alienation.

Despite the lack of institutions, which must be overcome gradually, the masses are now making history as a conscious collection of individuals fighting for the same cause. Man under socialism, despite his apparent standardization, is more complete. Despite the lack of a perfect mechanism for it, his opportunities for expressing himself and making himself felt in the social organism are infinitely greater.

It is still necessary to deepen his conscious participation, individual and collective, in all the mechanisms of management and production, and to link this to the idea of the need for technical and ideological education, so that he sees how closely interdependent these processes are and how their advancement is parallel. In this way he will reach total consciousness of his social being, which is equivalent to his full realization as a human creature, once the chains of alienation are broken.

This will be translated concretely into the reconquering of his true nature through liberated labor, and the expression of his own human condition through culture and art.

In order for him to develop in the first way, work must acquire a new status. Man-as-a-commodity ceases to exist, and a system is installed that establishes a quota for the fulfillment of his social duty. The means of production belong to society, and the machine is merely the trench where duty is fulfilled.

Man begins to free his thinking of the annoying fact that

he needs to work to satisfy his animal needs. He starts to see himself reflected in his work and to understand his full stature as a human being through the object created, through the work accomplished. Work no longer entails surrendering a part of his being in the form of labor power sold, which no longer belongs to him, but represents an emanation of himself, a contribution to the common life in which he is reflected, the fulfillment of his social duty.

We are doing everything possible to give work this new status of social duty and to link it on the one side with the development of technology, which will create the conditions for greater freedom, and on the other side with voluntary work based on the Marxist appreciation that man truly reaches his full human condition when he produces without being compelled by physical necessity to sell himself as a commodity.

Of course, there are still coercive aspects to work, even when it is voluntary. Man has not transformed all the coercion that surrounds him into conditioned reflexes of a social character, and in many cases he still produces under the pressures of his environment. (Fidel calls this moral compulsion.) He still needs to undergo a complete spiritual rebirth in his attitude toward his own work, freed from the direct pressure of his social environment, though linked to it by his new habits. That will be communism.

The change in consciousness does not take place automatically, just as change in the economy does not take place automatically. The alterations are slow and are not rhythmic; there are periods of acceleration, ones that are slower, and even retrogressions.

Furthermore we must take into account, as I pointed out before, that we are not dealing with a period of pure transition, as Marx envisaged it in his *Critique of the Gotha Program,* but rather with a new phase unforeseen by him: an initial period of the transition to communism, or of the construction of socialism. It is taking place in the midst of violent class struggles, and with elements of capitalism within it that obscure a complete understanding of its essence.

If we add to this the scholasticism that has held back the development of Marxist philosophy and impeded a systematic treatment of the transition period, whose political economy has not been developed, we must agree that we are still in diapers and that it is necessary to devote ourselves to investigating all the principal characteristics of this period before elaborating an economic and political theory of greater scope.

The resulting theory will, no doubt, put great stress on the two pillars of the construction of socialism: the education of the new man and the development of technology. Much remains to be done in regard to both, but delay is least excusable in regard to the concept of technology as a basic foundation since this is not a question of going forward blindly but of following a long stretch of road already opened up by the world's more advanced countries. This is why Fidel pounds away with such insistence on the need for the technological and scientific training of our people and especially of its vanguard.

In the field of ideas that do not lead to activities involving production, it is easier to see the division between material and spiritual necessity. For a long time man has been trying to free himself from alienation through culture and art. While he dies every day during the eight or more hours in which he functions as a commodity, he comes to life afterward in his spiritual creations. But this remedy bears the germs of the same sickness: it is a solitary individual seeking harmony with the world. He defends his individuality, which is oppressed by the environment, and reacts to aesthetic ideas as a unique being whose aspiration is to remain immaculate.

It is nothing more than an attempt to escape. The law

of value is no longer simply a reflection of the relations of production; the monopoly capitalists—even while employing purely empirical methods—surround it with a complicated scaffolding that turns it into a docile servant. The superstructure demands a kind of art that the artist has to be educated in. Rebels are subdued by the machine, and only exceptional talents may create their own work. The rest become shamefaced hirelings or are crushed.

A school of artistic inquiry is invented, which is said to be the definition of freedom, but this "inquiry" has its limits, imperceptible until we clash with them, that is, until the real problems of man and his alienation arise. Meaningless anguish or vulgar amusement thus become convenient safety valves for human anxiety. The idea of using art as a weapon of protest is combated.

Those who play by the rules of the game are showered with honors—such honors as a monkey might get for performing pirouettes. The condition is that you not try to escape from the invisible cage.

When the revolution took power there was an exodus of those who had been completely housebroken. The rest—whether they were revolutionaries or not—saw a new road. Artistic inquiry experienced a new impulse. The paths, however, had already been more or less laid out, and the escapist concept hid itself behind the word "freedom." This attitude was often found even among the revolutionaries themselves, a reflection in their consciousness of bourgeois idealism.

In countries that have gone through a similar process, attempts have been made to combat such tendencies by an exaggerated dogmatism. General culture was virtually a taboo, and the acme of cultural aspiration was declared to be the formally exact representation of nature. This was later transformed into a mechanical representation of the social reality they wanted to show: the ideal society, almost without conflicts or contradictions, that they sought to create.

Socialism is young and has its mistakes. We revolutionaries often lack the knowledge and intellectual daring needed to meet the task of developing the new man with methods different from the conventional ones—and the conventional methods suffer from the influences of the society that created them. (Again the theme of the relationship between form and content is posed.) Disorientation is widespread, and we are absorbed by the problems of material construction. There are no artists of great authority who at the same time have great revolutionary authority. The men of the party must take this task in hand and seek attainment of the main goal: to educate the people.

What is sought then is simplification, something everyone can understand, something functionaries understand. True artistic inquiry ends, and the problem of general culture is reduced to taking some things from the socialist present and some from the dead (therefore, not dangerous) past. Thus socialist realism arises upon the foundations of the art of the last century.

But the realistic art of the nineteenth century also has a class character, more purely capitalist perhaps than this decadent art of the twentieth century that reveals the anguish of alienated man. In the field of culture capitalism has given all that it had to give, and nothing remains but the stench of a corpse, today's decadence in art.

But why try to find the only valid prescription in the frozen forms of socialist realism? We cannot counterpose "freedom" to socialist realism, because the former does not yet exist and will not exist until the complete development of the new society. But we must not, from the pontifical throne of realism-at-all-costs, condemn all art forms since the first half of the nineteenth century, for we would then fall into the Proudhonian mistake of going back to the past, of putting a straitjacket on the artistic expression of the man who is being born and is in the process of making himself.

What is needed is the development of an ideological-cultural mechanism that permits both free inquiry and the uprooting of the weeds that multiply so easily in the fertilized soil of state subsidies.

In our country the error of mechanical realism has not appeared, but rather its opposite. And that is so because the need for the creation of a new man has not been understood, a new man who would represent neither the ideas of the nineteenth century nor those of our own decadent and morbid century.

What we must create is the man of the twenty-first century, although this is still a subjective aspiration, not yet systematized. This is precisely one of the fundamental objectives of our study and our work. To the extent that we achieve concrete successes on a theoretical plane—or, vice versa, to the extent that we draw theoretical conclusions of a broad character on the basis of our concrete research—we will have made a valuable contribution to Marxism-Leninism, to the cause of humanity.

By reacting against the man of the nineteenth century we have relapsed into the decadence of the twentieth century. It is not a very grave error, but we must overcome it lest we open a wide breach for revisionism.

The great multitudes continue to develop. The new ideas are gaining a good momentum within society. The material possibilities for the integrated development of absolutely all members of society make the task much more fruitful. The present is a time of struggle; the future is ours.

To sum up, the fault of many of our artists and intellectuals lies in their original sin: they are not truly revolutionaries. We can try to graft the elm tree so that it will bear pears, but at the same time we must plant pear trees. New generations will come that will be free of original sin. The probabilities that great artists will appear will be greater to the degree that the field of culture and the possibilities for expression are broadened.

Our task is to prevent the current generation, torn asunder by its conflicts, from becoming perverted and from perverting new generations. We must not create either docile servants of official thought, or "scholarship students" who live at the expense of the state—practicing freedom in quotation marks. Revolutionaries will come who will sing the song of the new man in the true voice of the people. That is a process that takes time.

In our society the youth and the party play a big part.

The former is especially important because it is the malleable clay from which the new man can be built without any of the old vestiges. The youth are treated in accordance with our aspirations. Their education is every day more complete, and we are not forgetting about their integration into work from the outset. Our scholarship students do physical work during their vacations or along with their studying. Work is a reward in some cases, a means of education in others, but it is never a punishment. A new generation is being born.

The party is a vanguard organization. It is made up of the best workers, who are proposed for membership by their fellow workers. It is a minority, but it has great authority because of the quality of its cadres. Our aspiration is for the party to become a mass party, but only when the masses have reached the level of the vanguard, that is, when they are educated for communism.

Our work constantly aims at this education. The party is the living example. Its cadres must teach hard work and sacrifice. By their action, they must lead the masses to the completion of the revolutionary task, and this involves years of hard struggle against the difficulties of construction, class enemies, the maladies of the past, imperialism.

I would now like to explain the role played by the individual, by man as an individual within the masses who make history. This is our experience; it is not a prescription.

Fidel gave the revolution its impulse in the first years, and also its leadership. He always set its tone. But there is a good group of revolutionaries who are developing along the same road as the central leader. And there is a great mass that follows its leaders because it has faith in them. It has faith in them because they have known how to interpret its aspirations.

It is not a matter of how many kilograms of meat one has to eat, nor of how many times a year someone can go to the beach, nor how many pretty things from abroad you might be able to buy with present-day wages. It is a matter of making the individual feel more complete, with much more internal richness and much more responsibility.

The individual in our country knows that the glorious period in which he happens to live is one of sacrifice; he is familiar with sacrifice. The first ones came to know it in the Sierra Maestra and wherever they fought; afterward all of Cuba came to know it. Cuba is the vanguard of Latin America and must make sacrifices because it occupies the post of advance guard, because it shows the masses of Latin America the road to full freedom.

Within the country the leadership has to carry out its vanguard role. And it must be said with all sincerity that in a real revolution, to which one gives his all and from which one expects no material reward, the task of the vanguard revolutionary is at one and the same time magnificent and agonizing.

At the risk of seeming ridiculous, let me say that the true revolutionary is guided by great feelings of love. It is impossible to think of a genuine revolutionary lacking this quality. Perhaps it is one of the great dramas of the leader that he must combine a passionate spirit with a cold intelligence and make painful decisions without flinching. Our vanguard revolutionaries must make an ideal of this love of the people, of the most sacred causes, and make it one and indivisible. They cannot descend, with small doses of daily affection, to the level where ordinary men put their love into practice.

The leaders of the revolution have children just beginning to talk, who are not learning to say "daddy." They have wives who must be part of the general sacrifice of their lives in order to take the revolution to its destiny. The circle of their friends is limited strictly to the circle of comrades in the revolution. There is no life outside of it.

In these circumstances one must have a big dose of humanity, a big dose of a sense of justice and truth in order not to fall into dogmatic extremes, into cold scholasticism, into an isolation from the masses. We must strive every day so that this love of living humanity is transformed into actual deeds, into acts that serve as examples, as a moving force.

The revolutionary, the ideological motor force of the revolution within his party, is consumed by this uninterrupted activity that comes to an end only with death, unless the construction of socialism is accomplished on a world scale. If his revolutionary zeal is blunted when the most urgent tasks have been accomplished on a local scale and he forgets about proletarian internationalism, the revolution he leads will cease to be a driving force and sink into a comfortable drowsiness that imperialism, our irreconcilable enemy, will utilize to gain ground. Proletarian internationalism is a duty, but it is also a revolutionary necessity. This is the way we educate our people.

Of course there are dangers in the present situation, and not only that of dogmatism, not only that of freezing the ties with the masses midway in the great task. There is also the danger of the weaknesses we can fall into. If a man thinks that dedicating his entire life to the revolution means that in return he should not be distracted by such worries as that his child lacks certain things, that his children's shoes are worn out, that his family lacks some necessity, then with this reasoning he opens his mind to infection by the germs of future corruption.

In our case we have maintained that our children should have or should go without those things that the children of the common man have or go without, and that our families should understand this and struggle for it to be that way. The revolution is made through man, but man must forge his revolutionary spirit day by day.

Thus we march on. At the head of the immense column—we are neither ashamed nor afraid to say it—is Fidel. After him come the best cadres of the party, and immediately behind them, so close that we feel its tremendous force, comes the people in its entirety, a solid structure of individualities moving toward a common goal, individuals who have attained consciousness of what must be done, men who fight to escape from the realm of necessity and to enter that of freedom.

This great throng organizes itself; its organization is a result of its consciousness of the necessity of this organization. It is no longer a dispersed force, divisible into thousands of fragments thrown into the air like splinters from a hand grenade, trying by any means to achieve some protection from an uncertain future, in desperate struggle with their fellows.

We know that sacrifices lie ahead and that we must pay a price for the heroic fact that we are, as a nation, a vanguard. We, as leaders, know that we must pay a price for the right to say that we are at the head of a people that is at the head of Latin America. Each and every one of us punctually pays his quota of sacrifice, conscious of being rewarded with the satisfaction of fulfilling a duty, conscious of advancing with everyone toward the new man visible on the horizon.

Allow me to draw some conclusions:

We socialists are freer because we are more complete; we are more complete because we are freer.

The skeleton of our complete freedom is already formed. The flesh and the clothing are lacking; we will create them.

Our freedom and its daily sustenance are paid for in blood and sacrifice.

Our sacrifice is conscious: an installment payment on the freedom that we are building.

The road is long and in part unknown. We know our limitations. We will create the man of the twenty-first century—we, ourselves.

We will forge ourselves in daily action, creating a new man with a new technology.

The individual plays a role in mobilizing and leading the masses insofar as he embodies the highest virtues and aspirations of the people and does not wander from the path.

Clearing the way is the vanguard group, the best among the good, the party.

The basic clay of our work is the youth. We place our hope in them and prepare them to take the banner from our hands.

If this inarticulate letter clarifies anything, it has accomplished the objective that motivated it. Receive our ritual greeting—which is like a handshake or an *"Ave María Purísima"*:

Patria o muerte!

Farewell letter to Fidel

Though Guevara had returned to Cuba on March 14, 1965, his absence from public functions soon excited comment and, as the months went by, became an international mystery. Finally, on October 3, during the televised ceremony of the presentation of the newly established Central Committee of the Communist Party of Cuba, Castro, in the presence of Guevara's wife and children, read the following letter. Castro explained that the letter had been delivered to him back in April and that Guevara had left the timing of its disclosure to Castro's discretion. He had delayed so long in making it public out of concern for Guevara's security and, for the same reason, could not divulge his present whereabouts.

Havana
Year of Agriculture
Fidel:

At this moment I remember many things—when I met you in María Antonia's house, when you proposed I come along, all the tensions involved in the preparations. One day they came by and asked who should be notified in case of death, and the real possibility of it struck us all. Later we knew it was true, that in a revolution one wins or dies (if it is a real one). Many comrades fell along the way to victory.

Today everything has a less dramatic tone, because we are more mature, but the event repeats itself. I feel that I have fulfilled the part of my duty that tied me to the Cuban revolution in its territory, and I say farewell to you, to the comrades, to your people, who now are mine.

I formally resign my positions in the leadership of the party, my post as minister, my rank of commander, and my Cuban citizenship. Nothing legal binds me to Cuba. The only ties are of another nature—those that cannot be broken as can appointments to posts.

Reviewing my past life, I believe I have worked with sufficient integrity and dedication to consolidate the revolutionary triumph. My only serious failing was not having had more confidence in you from the first moments in the Sierra Maestra, and not having understood quickly enough your qualities as a leader and a revolutionary.

I have lived magnificent days, and at your side I felt the pride of belonging to our people in the brilliant yet sad days of the Caribbean crisis. Seldom has a statesman been more brilliant than you were in those days. I am also proud of having followed you without hesitation, of having identified with your way of thinking and of seeing and appraising dangers and principles.

Other nations of the world summon my modest efforts of assistance. I can do that which is denied you owing to your responsibility at the head of Cuba, and the time has come for us to part.

You should know that I do so with a mixture of joy and sorrow. I leave here the purest of my hopes as a builder and the dearest of those I hold dear. And I leave a people who received me as a son. That wounds a part of my spirit. I carry to new battlefronts the faith that you taught me, the revolutionary spirit of my people, the feeling of fulfilling the most sacred of duties: to fight against imperialism wherever one may be. This is a source of strength, and more than heals the deepest of wounds.

I state once more that I free Cuba from all responsibility, except that which stems from its example. If my final hour finds me under other skies, my last thought will be of this people and especially of you. I am grateful for your teaching and your example, to which I shall try to be faithful up to the final consequences of my acts.

I have always been identified with the foreign policy of our revolution, and I continue to be. Wherever I am, I will feel the responsibility of being a Cuban revolutionary, and I shall behave as such. I am not sorry that I leave nothing material to my wife and children; I am happy it is that way. I ask nothing for them, as the state will provide them with enough to live on and receive an education.

I would have many things to say to you and to our people, but I feel they are unnecessary. Words cannot express what I would like them to, and there is no point in scribbling pages.

Hasta la victoria siempre! [Ever onward to victory!]

Patria o muerte!

I embrace you with all my revolutionary fervor.

Che

Farewell letter to his parents

When Castro read Guevara's letter of farewell, he said that the absent revolutionist had in the same period written farewell letters to his family and to various comrades and that they would be asked "to donate them to the revolution because we consider that they are documents worthy of being part of history." One of these, a letter to his parents which was published in Cuba in 1967, appears below.

Dear folks:

Once again I feel beneath my heels the ribs of Rocinante. Once more, I'm on the road with my shield on my arm. Almost ten years ago, I wrote you another farewell letter. As I recall, I lamented not being a better soldier and a better doctor. The latter no longer interests me; I am not such a bad soldier.

Nothing has changed in essence, except that I am much more conscious. My Marxism has taken root and become purified. I believe in armed struggle as the only solution for those peoples who fight to free themselves, and I am consistent with my beliefs. Many will call me an adventurer, and that I am—only one of a different sort: one who risks his skin to prove his truths.

It is possible that this may be the end. I don't seek it, but it's within the logical realm of probabilities. If it should be so, I send you a final embrace. I have loved you very much, only I have not known how to express my affection. I am extremely rigid in my actions, and I think that sometimes you did not understand me. It was not easy to understand me. Nevertheless, please believe me today.

Now a willpower that I have polished with an artist's delight will sustain some shaky legs and some weary lungs. I will do it.

Give a thought once in a while to this little soldier of fortune of the twentieth century.

A kiss to Celia, to Roberto, Juan Martín and Patotín, to Beatriz, to everybody. For you, a big hug from your obstinate and prodigal son,

Ernesto

Vietnam and the world struggle for freedom

In the interval between his disappearance from Cuba in the spring of 1965 and his death in Bolivia in the fall of 1967, Guevara made one public statement. It was his message "from somewhere in the world" to the Organization of Solidarity of the Peoples of Africa, Asia and Latin America. It was made public in Havana by the news service Prensa Latina on April 16, 1967. It is presented here in full.

"It is the hour of the furnace, and the light is all that can be seen."

JOSÉ MARTÍ

Twenty-one years have elapsed since the end of the last world conflagration, and various publications in every language are celebrating this event, symbolized by the defeat of Japan. A climate of optimism is apparent in many sectors of the different camps into which the world is divided.

Twenty-one years without a world war in these days of

maximum confrontations, of violent clashes and abrupt turns, appears to be a very high number. All of us declare our readiness to fight for this peace. But without analyzing its practical results (poverty, degradation, constantly increasing exploitation of enormous sectors of humanity), it is appropriate to ask whether this peace is real.

The purpose of these notes is not to write the history of the various conflicts of a local character that have followed one after another since Japan's surrender. Nor is it our task to recount the numerous and growing instances of civil strife that have occurred in these years of supposed peace. It is enough to point to the wars in Korea and Vietnam as examples to counter the boundless optimism.

In Korea, after years of ferocious struggle, the northern part of the country was left submerged in the most terrible devastation in the annals of modern war: riddled with bombs; without factories, schools, or hospitals; without any kind of housing to shelter 10 million inhabitants.

Dozens of countries intervened in that war, led militarily by the United States, under the false banner of the United Nations, with the massive participation of U.S. troops and the use of the conscripted South Korean people as cannon fodder. On the other side, the army and people of Korea and the volunteers from the People's Republic of China received supplies and advice from the Soviet military apparatus. The United States carried out all kinds of tests of weapons of destruction, excluding thermonuclear ones, but including bacteriological and chemical weapons on a limited scale.

In Vietnam a war has been waged almost without interruption by the patriotic forces of that country against three imperialist powers: Japan, whose might plummeted after the bombings of Hiroshima and Nagasaki; France, which recovered its Indochinese colonies from that defeated country, disregarding the promises made at a time of duress; and the United States, in the latest phase of the conflict.

There have been limited confrontations on all continents, even though on the Latin American continent there were for a long time only attempts at freedom struggles and military coups d'état, until the Cuban revolution sounded its clarion call, signaling the importance of this region and attracting the wrath of the imperialists, compelling Cuba to defend its coasts first at Playa Girón and then during the October crisis.

The latter incident could have touched off a war of incalculable proportions if a U.S.-Soviet clash had occurred over the Cuban question.

Right now, however, the contradictions are clearly centered in the territories of the Indochinese peninsula and the neighboring countries. Laos and Vietnam were shaken by conflicts that ceased to be civil wars when U.S. imperialism intervened with all its power, and the whole region became a lit fuse, leading to a powder keg. In Vietnam the confrontation has taken on an extremely sharp character. It is not our intention to go into the history of this war either. We will just point out some milestones.

In 1954, after the crushing defeat [of the French forces] at Dien Bien Phu, the Geneva accords were signed, dividing Vietnam into two zones with the stipulation that elections would be held in eighteen months to determine who would govern the country and how it would be reunified. The United States did not sign that document, but began maneuvering to replace Emperor Bao Dai, a French puppet, with a man who fit their aims. He turned out to be Ngo Dinh Diem, whose tragic end—that of a lemon squeezed dry by imperialism—is known to everyone.

In the months following the signing of the accords, optimism reigned in the camp of the popular forces. They dismantled military positions of the anti-French struggle in the southern part of the country and waited for the agreement to be carried out. But the patriots soon realized that there would be no elections unless the United States felt capable of imposing its will at the ballot box, something it could not do even with all its methods of electoral fraud.

The struggles in the southern part of the country began once again, and these have been gaining in intensity. Today the U.S. army has grown to almost a half-million invaders, while the puppet forces decline in number and, above all, have totally lost the will to fight.

It has been about two years since the United States began the systematic bombing of the Democratic Republic of Vietnam in yet another attempt to halt the fighting spirit in the South and to impose a conference from a position of strength. At the beginning, the bombings were more or less isolated occurrences, carried out in the guise of reprisals for alleged provocations from the North. Then their intensity and regularity increased, until they became one gigantic onslaught by the U.S. air force carried out day after day, with the purpose of destroying every vestige of civilization in the northern zone of the country. It is one episode in the sadly notorious escalation.

The material aims of the Yankee world have been achieved in good part despite the valiant defense put up by the Vietnamese antiaircraft batteries, the more than 1,700 planes brought down, and the aid in military supplies from the socialist camp.

This is the painful reality: Vietnam, a nation representing the aspirations and hopes for victory of all the world's disinherited, is tragically alone. This people must endure the pounding of U.S. technology—in the south almost without defenses, in the north with some possibilities of defense—but always alone.

The solidarity of the progressive world with the Vietnamese people has something of the bitter irony of the plebeians cheering on the gladiators in the Roman Circus. To wish the victim success is not enough; one must share his fate. One must join him in death or in victory.

When we analyze the isolation of the Vietnamese, we are overcome by anguish at this illogical moment in the history of humanity. U.S. imperialism is guilty of aggression. Its crimes are immense, extending over the whole world. We know this, gentlemen! But also guilty are those who at the decisive moment hesitated to make Vietnam an inviolable part of socialist territory—yes, at the risk of a war of global scale, but also compelling the U.S. imperialists to make a decision. And also guilty are those who persist in a war of insults and tripping each other up, begun quite some time ago by the representatives of the two biggest powers in the socialist camp.

Let us ask, seeking an honest answer: Is Vietnam isolated or not, as it tries to maintain a dangerous balancing act between the two quarreling powers?

And what greatness has been shown by this people! What a stoic and courageous people! And what a lesson for the world their struggle holds.

It will be a long time before we know if President Johnson ever seriously intended to initiate some of the reforms needed by his people—to sandpaper the class contradictions that are appearing with explosive force and mounting frequency. What is certain is that the improvements announced under the pompous title of the Great Society have gone down the drain in Vietnam. The greatest of the imperialist powers is feeling in its own bowels the bleeding inflicted by a poor, backward country; its fabulous economy is strained by the war effort. Killing has ceased to be the most comfortable business for the monopolies.

Defensive weapons, and not in sufficient number, are all these marvelous Vietnamese soldiers have besides love for their country, for their society, and a courage that stands up to all tests. But imperialism is bogged down in Vietnam. It sees no way out and is searching desperately for one that will permit it to emerge with dignity from the dangerous situation in which it finds itself. The "four points" put forward by the North and the "five" by the South have it caught in a pincers, however, making the confrontation still more decisive.

Everything seems to indicate that peace, the precarious peace that bears that name only because no global conflagration has occurred, is again in danger of being broken by some irreversible and unacceptable step taken by the United States.

What is the role that we, the exploited of the world, must play?

The peoples of three continents are watching and learning a lesson for themselves in Vietnam. Since the imperialists are using the threat of war to blackmail humanity, the correct response is not to fear war. Attack hard and without letup at every point of confrontation—that must be the general tactic of the peoples.

But in those places where this miserable peace that we endure has not been broken, what shall our task be?

To liberate ourselves at any price.

The world panorama is one of great complexity. The task of winning liberation still lies ahead even for some countries of old Europe, sufficiently developed to experience all the contradictions of capitalism but so weak that they can no longer follow the course of imperialism or embark on that road. In those countries the contradictions will become explosive in the coming years. But their problems, and hence their solutions, are different from those facing our dependent and economically backward peoples.

The fundamental field of imperialist exploitation covers the three backward continents—Latin America, Asia, and Africa. Each country has its own characteristics, but the continents, as a whole, have their own as well.

Latin America constitutes a more or less homogeneous

whole, and in almost its entire territory U.S. monopoly capital holds absolute primacy. The puppet—or, in the best of cases—weak and timid governments are unable to resist the orders of the Yankee master. The United States has reached virtually the pinnacle of its political and economic domination. There is little room left for it to advance; any change in the situation could turn into a step backward from its primacy. Its policy is to maintain its conquests. The course of action is reduced at the present time to the brutal use of force to prevent liberation movements of any kind.

Behind the slogan "We will not permit another Cuba" hides the possibility of cowardly acts of aggression they can get away with—such as the one against the Dominican Republic; or, before that, the massacre in Panama and the clear warning that Yankee troops are ready to intervene anywhere in Latin America where a change in the established order endangers their interests. This policy enjoys almost absolute impunity. The OAS [Organization of American States] is a convenient mask, no matter how discredited it is. The UN's ineffectiveness borders on the ridiculous or the tragic. The armies of all the countries of Latin America are ready to intervene to crush their own people. What has been formed, in fact, is the International of Crime and Betrayal.

On the other hand, the indigenous bourgeoisies have lost all capacity to oppose imperialism—if they ever had any—and are only dragged along behind it like a caboose. There are no other alternatives. Either a socialist revolution or a caricature of revolution.

Asia is a continent with different characteristics. The liberation struggles against a series of European colonial powers resulted in the establishment of more or less progressive governments, whose subsequent evolution has in some cases deepened the main objectives of national liberation, and in others reverted toward proimperialist positions.

From the economic point of view, the United States had

little to lose and much to gain in Asia. Changes work to its favor; it is struggling to displace other neocolonial powers, to penetrate new spheres of action in the economic field, sometimes directly, sometimes utilizing Japan.

But special political conditions exist there, above all in the Indochinese peninsula, that give Asia characteristics of major importance and that play an important role in the global military strategy of U.S. imperialism. The latter is imposing a blockade around China utilizing South Korea, Japan, Taiwan, South Vietnam, and Thailand, at a minimum.

This dual situation—a strategic interest as important as the military blockade of the People's Republic of China, and the ambition of U.S. capital to penetrate those big markets it does not yet dominate—makes Asia one of the most explosive places in the world today, despite the apparent stability outside of the Vietnamese area.

Belonging geographically to this continent, but with its own contradictions, the Middle East is at the boiling point. It is not possible to foresee what the cold war between Israel, which is backed by the imperialists, and the progressive countries of this region will lead to. It is another one of the threatening volcanoes in the world.

Africa appears almost like virgin territory for neocolonial invasion. Changes have occurred that, to a certain degree, have compelled the neocolonial powers to give up their former absolute prerogatives. But when the processes continue without interruption to their conclusion, colonialism gives way without violence to a neocolonialism, with the same consequences in regard to economic domination.

The United States did not have colonies in this region and is now struggling to penetrate its partners' old private preserves. It can be said with certainty that Africa constitutes a long-term reservoir in the strategic plans of U.S. imperialism. Its current investments there are of importance only in the Union of South Africa, and it is beginning its penetration of the Congo, Nigeria, and other countries, where a violent competition is opening up (of a peaceful nature up to now) with other imperialist powers. It does not yet have big interests to defend except its alleged right to intervene any place on the globe where its monopolies smell good profits or the existence of big reserves of raw materials. All this background makes it legitimate to pose a question about the possibilities for the liberation of the peoples in the short or medium term.

If we analyze Africa, we see that there are struggles of some intensity in the Portuguese colonies of Guinea, Mozambique, and Angola, with particular success in Guinea and varying successes in the other two. We are also still witnessing a struggle between Lumumba's successors and the old accomplices of Tshombe in the Congo, a struggle that appears at the moment to be leaning in favor of the latter, who have "pacified" a big part of the country for their benefit, although war remains latent.

In Rhodesia the problem is different: British imperialism used all the means at its disposal to hand power over to the white minority, which now holds it. The conflict, from England's point of view, is absolutely not official. This Western power, with its usual diplomatic cleverness—in plain language also called hypocrisy—presents a facade of displeasure with the measures adopted by the government of Ian Smith. It is supported in this sly attitude by some Commonwealth countries that follow it, but is attacked by a good number of the countries of Black Africa, even those that are docile economic vassals of British imperialism.

In Rhodesia the situation could become highly explosive if the efforts of the Black patriots to rise up in arms were to crystallize and if this movement were effectively supported by the neighboring African nations. But for now all these problems are being aired in bodies as innocuous as the UN, the Commonwealth, or the Organization of African Unity.

Nevertheless, the political and social evolution of Africa does not lead us to foresee a continental revolutionary situation. The liberation struggles against the Portuguese must end victoriously, but Portugal signifies nothing on the imperialist roster. The confrontations of revolutionary importance are those that put the whole imperialist apparatus in check, although we will not for that reason cease struggling for the liberation of the three Portuguese colonies and for the deepening of their revolutions.

When the Black masses of South Africa or Rhodesia begin their genuine revolutionary struggle, a new era will have opened in Africa. Or, when the impoverished masses of a country set out against the ruling oligarchies to conquer their right to a decent life. Up to now there has been a succession of barracks coups, in which one group of officers replaces another or replaces a ruler who no longer serves their caste interests and those of the powers that control them behind the scenes. But there have been no popular upheavals. In the Congo these characteristics were fleetingly present, inspired by the memory of Lumumba, but they have been losing strength in recent months.

In Asia, as we have seen, the situation is explosive, and Vietnam and Laos, where the struggle is now going on, are not the only points of friction. The same holds true for Cambodia, where at any moment the United States might launch a direct attack. We should add Thailand, Malaysia, and, of course, Indonesia, where we cannot believe that the final word has been spoken despite the annihilation of the Communist Party of that country after the reactionaries took power. And, of course, the Middle East.

In Latin America, the struggle is going on arms in hand in Guatemala, Colombia, Venezuela, and Bolivia, and the first outbreaks are already beginning in Brazil. Other centers of resistance have appeared and been extinguished. But almost all the countries of this continent are ripe for a struggle of the kind that, to be triumphant, cannot settle for anything less than the establishment of a government of a socialist nature.

In this continent virtually one language only is spoken save for the exceptional case of Brazil, with whose people Spanish-speakers can communicate in view of the similarity between the two languages. There is such a similarity between the classes in these countries that they have an "international American" type of identification, much more so than in other continents. Language, customs, religion, a common master, unite them. The degree and forms of exploitation are similar in their effects for exploiters and exploited in a good number of countries of our America. And within it rebellion is ripening at an accelerated rate.

We may ask: This rebellion—how will it bear fruit? What kind of rebellion will it be? We have maintained for some time that given its similar characteristics, the struggle in Latin America will in due time acquire continental dimensions. It will be the scene of many great battles waged by humanity for its own liberation.

In the framework of this struggle of continental scope, the ones that are currently being carried on in an active way are only episodes. But they have already provided martyrs who will figure in the history of the Americas as having given their necessary quota of blood for this final stage in the struggle for the full freedom of man. There are the names of Commander Turcios Lima, the priest Camilo Torres, Commander Fabricio Ojeda, Commanders Lobatón and Luis de la Puente Uceda, central figures in the revolutionary movements of Guatemala, Colombia, Venezuela, and Peru.

But the active mobilization of the people creates its new leaders—César Montes and Yon Sosa are raising the banner in Guatemala; Fabio Vázquez and Marulanda are doing it in Colombia; Douglas Bravo in the western part of the country and Américo Martín in El Bachiller are leading their respective fronts in Venezuela.

New outbreaks of war will appear in these and other Latin American countries, as has already occurred in Bolivia. And they will continue to grow, with all the vicissitudes involved in this dangerous occupation of the modern revolutionist. Many will die, victims of their own errors; others will fall in the difficult combat to come; new fighters and new leaders will arise in the heat of the revolutionary struggle.

The people will create their fighters and their leaders along the way in the selective framework of the war itself, and the Yankee agents of repression will increase in number. Today there are advisers in all countries where armed struggle is going on. It seems that the Peruvian army, also advised and trained by the Yankees, carried out a successful attack on the revolutionists of that country. But if the guerrilla centers are led with sufficient political and military skill, they will become practically unbeatable and will make necessary new reinforcements by the Yankees. In Peru itself, with tenacity and firmness, new figures, although not yet fully known, are reorganizing the guerrilla struggle.

Little by little, the obsolete weapons that suffice to repress the small armed bands will turn into modern weapons, and the groups of advisers into U.S. combatants, until at a certain point they find themselves obliged to send growing numbers of regular troops to secure the relative stability of a power whose national puppet army is disintegrating in the face of the guerrillas' struggles.

This is the road of Vietnam. It is the road that the peoples must follow. It is the road that Latin America will follow, with the special feature that the armed groups might establish something such as coordinating committees to make the repressive tasks of Yankee imperialism more difficult and to help their own cause.

Latin America—a continent forgotten in the recent political struggles for liberation, which is beginning to make itself felt through the Tricontinental in the voice of the vanguard of its peoples: the Cuban revolution—will have a much more important task: the creation of the world's second or third Vietnam, or second *and* third Vietnam.

We must keep in mind at all times that imperialism is a world system, the final stage of capitalism, and that it must be beaten in a great worldwide confrontation. The strategic objective of that struggle must be the destruction of imperialism.

The contribution that falls to us, the exploited and backward of the world, is to eliminate the foundations sustaining imperialism: our oppressed nations, from which capital, raw materials, and cheap labor (both workers and technicians) are extracted, and to which new capital (tools of domination), arms, and all kinds of goods are exported, sinking us into absolute dependence. The fundamental element of that strategic objective, then, will be the real liberation of the peoples, a liberation that will be the result of armed struggle in the majority of cases, and that, in Latin America, will almost unfailingly turn into a socialist revolution.

In focusing on the destruction of imperialism, it is necessary to identify its head, which is none other than the United States of North America.

We must carry out a task of a general kind, the tactical aim of which is to draw the enemy out of his environment, compelling him to fight in places where his living habits clash with existing conditions. The adversary must not be underestimated; the U.S. soldier has technical ability and is backed by means of such magnitude as to make him formidable. What he lacks essentially is the ideological motivation, which his most hated rivals of today—the Vietnamese soldiers—have to the highest degree. We will be able to triumph over this army only to the extent that we succeed in undermining its morale. And this is done by inflicting defeats on it and causing it repeated sufferings.

But this brief outline for victories entails immense sacrifices by the peoples—sacrifices that must be demanded starting right now, in the light of day, and that will perhaps be less painful than those they would have to endure if we constantly avoided battle in an effort to get others to pull the chestnuts out of the fire for us.

Clearly, the last country to free itself will very probably do so without an armed struggle, and its people will be spared the suffering of a long war as cruel as imperialist wars are. But it may be impossible to avoid this struggle or its effects in a conflict of worldwide character, and the suffering may be as much or greater. We cannot predict the future, but we must never give way to the cowardly temptation to be the standard-bearers of a people who yearn for freedom but renounce the struggle that goes with it, and who wait as if expecting it to come as the crumbs of victory.

It is absolutely correct to avoid any needless sacrifice. That is why it is so important to be clear on the real possibilities that dependent Latin America has to free itself in a peaceful way. For us the answer to this question is clear: now may or may not be the right moment to start the struggle, but we can have no illusions, nor do we have a right to believe, that freedom can be won without a fight.

And the battles will not be mere street fights with stones against tear gas, nor peaceful general strikes. Nor will it be the struggle of an infuriated people that destroys the repressive apparatus of the ruling oligarchies in two or three days. It will be a long, bloody struggle in which the front will be in guerrilla refuges in the cities, in the homes of the combatants (where the repression will go seeking easy victims among their families), among the massacred peasant population, in the towns or cities destroyed by the enemy's bombs.

We are being pushed into this struggle. It cannot be remedied other than by preparing for it and deciding to undertake it.

The beginning will not be easy; it will be extremely difficult. All the oligarchies' repressive capacity, all its capacity for demagogy and brutality will be placed in the service of its cause.

Our mission, in the first hour, is to survive; then, to act, the perennial example of the guerrilla carrying on armed propaganda in the Vietnamese meaning of the term, that is, the propaganda of bullets, of battles that are won or lost—but that are waged—against the enemy.

The great lesson of the guerrillas' invincibility is taking hold among the masses of the dispossessed. The galvanization of the national spirit; the preparation for more difficult tasks, for resistance to more violent repression. Hate as a factor in the struggle, intransigent hatred for the enemy that takes one beyond the natural limitations of a human being and converts one into an effective, violent, selective, cold, killing machine. Our soldiers must be like that; a people without hate cannot triumph over a brutal enemy.

We must carry the war as far as the enemy carries it: into his home, into his places of recreation, make it total. He must be prevented from having a moment's peace, a moment's quiet outside the barracks and even inside them. Attack him wherever he may be; make him feel like a hunted animal wherever he goes. Then his morale will begin to decline. He will become even more bestial, but the signs of the coming decline will appear.

And let us develop genuine proletarian internationalism, with international proletarian armies. Let the flag under which we fight be the sacred cause of the liberation of humanity, so that to die under the colors of Vietnam, Venezuela, Guatemala, Laos, Guinea, Colombia, Bolivia, Brazil—to mention only the current scenes of armed struggle—will be equally glorious and desirable for a Latin American, an Asian, an African, and even a European.

Every drop of blood spilled in a land under whose flag

one was not born is experience gathered by the survivor to be applied later in the struggle for liberation of one's own country. And every people that liberates itself is a step in the battle for the liberation of one's own people.

It is time to moderate our disputes and place everything at the service of the struggle.

That big controversies are agitating the world that is struggling for freedom, all of us know; we cannot hide that. That these controversies have acquired a character and a sharpness that make dialogue and reconciliation appear extremely difficult, if not impossible, we know that too. To seek ways to initiate a dialogue avoided by those in dispute is a useless task.

But the enemy is there, it strikes day after day and threatens new blows, and these blows will unite us today, tomorrow, or the next day. Whoever understands this first and prepares this necessary unity will win the peoples' gratitude.

In view of the virulence and intransigence with which each side argues its case, we, the dispossessed, cannot agree with either way these differences are expressed, even when we agree with some of the positions of one or the other side, or when we agree more with the positions of one or the other side. In this time of struggle, the way in which the current differences have been aired is a weakness. But given the situation, it is an illusion to think that the matter can be resolved through words. History will either sweep away these disputes or pass its final judgment on them.

In our world in struggle, everything related to disputes around tactics and methods of action for the attainment of limited objectives must be analyzed with the respect due others' opinions. As for the great strategic objective—the total destruction of imperialism by means of struggle—on that we must be intransigent.

Let us sum up as follows our aspirations for victory. Destruction of imperialism by means of eliminating its strongest bulwark: the imperialist domination of the United States of North America. To take as a tactical line the gradual liberation of the peoples, one by one or in groups, involving the enemy in a difficult struggle outside his terrain; destroying his bases of support, that is, his dependent territories.

This means a long war. And, we repeat once again, a cruel war. Let no one deceive himself when he sets out to begin, and let no one hesitate to begin out of fear of the results it can bring upon his own people. It is almost the only hope for victory.

We cannot evade the call of the hour. Vietnam teaches us this with its permanent lesson in heroism, its tragic daily lesson of struggle and death in order to gain the final victory.

Over there, the soldiers of imperialism encounter the discomforts of those who, accustomed to the standard of living that the United States boasts, have to confront a hostile land; the insecurity of those who cannot move without feeling that they are stepping on enemy territory; death for those who go outside of fortified compounds; the permanent hostility of the entire population. All this is provoking repercussions inside the United States. It is leading to the appearance of a factor that was attenuated by imperialism at full strength: the class struggle inside its own territory.

How close and bright would the future appear if two, three, many Vietnams flowered on the face of the globe, with their quota of death and their immense tragedies, with their daily heroism, with their repeated blows against imperialism, forcing it to disperse its forces under the lash of the growing hatred of the peoples of the world!

And if we were all capable of uniting in order to give our blows greater solidity and certainty, so that the aid of all kinds to the peoples in struggle was even more effective—how great the future would be, and how near!

If we, on a small point on the map of the world, fulfill our duty and place at the disposal of the struggle whatever little we are able to give—our lives, our sacrifice—it can happen that one of these days we will draw our last breath on a bit of earth not our own, yet already ours, watered with our blood. Let it be known that we have measured the scope of our acts and that we consider ourselves no more than a part of the great army of the proletariat. But we feel proud at having learned from the Cuban revolution and from its great main leader the great lesson to be drawn from its position in this part of the world: "Of what difference are the dangers to a man or a people, or the sacrifices they make, when what is at stake is the destiny of humanity?"

Our every action is a battle cry against imperialism and a call for the unity of the peoples against the great enemy of the human race: the United States of North America.

Wherever death may surprise us, let it be welcome if our battle cry has reached even one receptive ear, if another hand reaches out to take up our arms, and other men come forward to join in our funeral dirge with the rattling of machine guns and with new cries of battle and victory.

Index

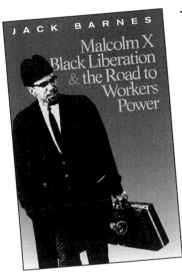

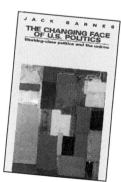

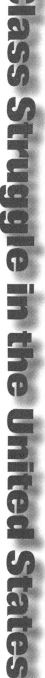

Class Struggle in the United States

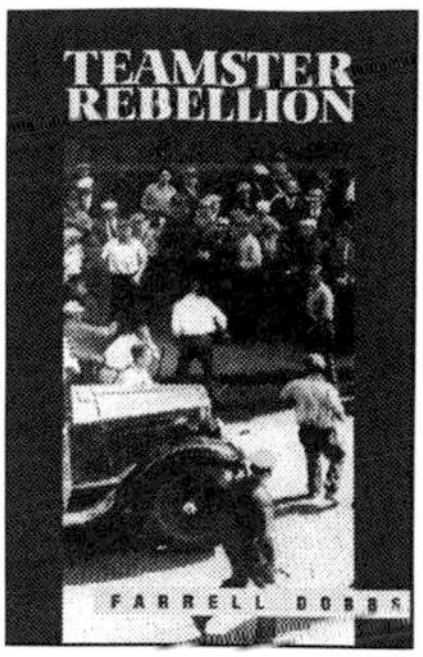

Teamster Rebellion

FARRELL DOBBS

The first of a four-volume participant's account of how strikes and organizing drives across the Midwest in the 1930s, initiated by leaders of Teamsters Local 574 in Minneapolis, paved the way for industrial unions and a fighting working-class social movement. These battles showed what workers and farmers can achieve when they have the leadership they deserve. Dobbs was a central part of that class-struggle leadership. $19. Also in Spanish, French, and Swedish.

Fighting Racism in World War II

From the Pages of the Militant

An account from 1939 to 1945 of struggles against racism and lynch-mob terror in face of patriotic appeals to postpone resistance until after US "victory" in World War II. These struggles—of a piece with anti-imperialist battles the world over—helped lay the basis for the mass Black rights movement in the 1950s and '60s. $25

The First Ten Years of American Communism

JAMES P. CANNON

A founding leader of the communist movement in the US recounts early efforts to build a proletarian party emulating the Bolshevik leadership of the October 1917 revolution in Russia. $22

Revolutionary Continuity

Marxist Leadership in the U.S.

FARRELL DOBBS

How successive generations of fighters joined in struggles that shaped the US labor movement, seeking to build a revolutionary leadership able to advance the interests of workers and small farmers and link up with fellow toilers worldwide. 2 vols. *The Early Years: 1848–1917*, $20; *Birth of the Communist Movement: 1918–1922*, $19.

The Cuban Revolution and

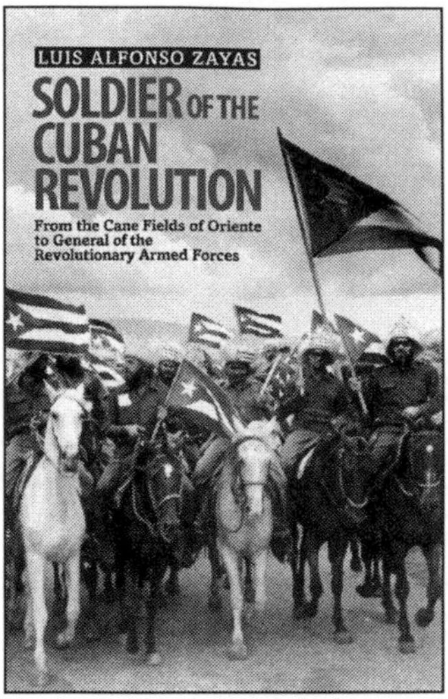

Soldier of the Cuban Revolution

From the Cane Fields of Oriente to General of the Revolutionary Armed Forces

Luis Alfonso Zayas

The author recounts his experiences over five decades in the revolution. From a teenage combatant in the clandestine struggle and 1956–58 war that brought down the US-backed dictatorship, to serving three times as a leader of the Cuban volunteer forces that helped Angola defeat an invasion by the army of white-supremacist South Africa, Zayas tells how he and other ordinary men and women in Cuba changed the course of history and, in the process, transformed themselves as well. $18. Also in Spanish.

Our History Is Still Being Written

The Story of Three Chinese-Cuban Generals in the Cuban Revolution

Armando Choy, Gustavo Chui, and Moisés Sío Wong talk about the historic place of Chinese immigration to Cuba, as well as more than five decades of revolutionary action and internationalism, from Cuba to Angola and Venezuela today. Through their stories we see how millions of ordinary men and women opened the door to socialist revolution in the Americas, changed the course of history, and became different human beings in the process. $20. Also in Spanish and Chinese.

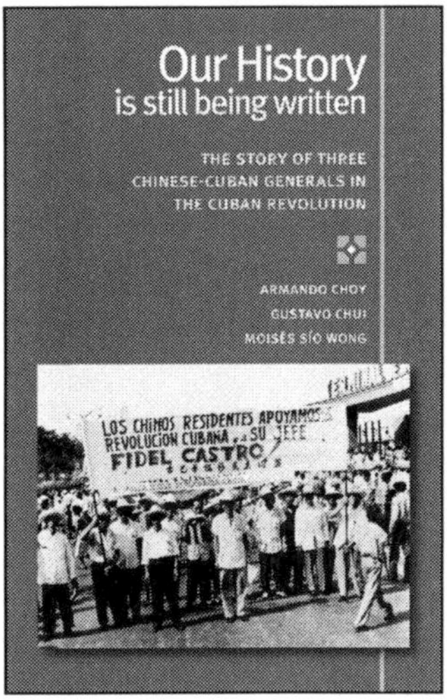

Marianas in Combat

Teté Puebla and the Mariana Grajales Women's Platoon in Cuba's Revolutionary War 1956–58

Teté Puebla

Brigadier General Teté Puebla joined the struggle to overthrow the US-backed Batista dictatorship in Cuba in 1956, at age fifteen. This is her story—from clandestine action in the cities, to officer in the Rebel Army's first all-women's platoon. The fight to transform the social and economic status of women is inseparable from Cuba's socialist revolution. $14. Also in Spanish.

World Politics

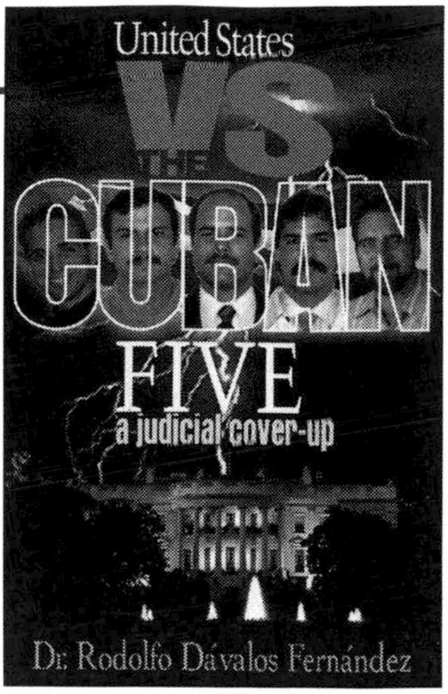

United States vs. The Cuban Five

A Judicial Cover-Up

Rodolfo Dávalos Fernández

Held in US prisons since 1998, five Cuban revolutionists were framed up for being part of a "Cuban spy network" in Florida. They were keeping tabs for Cuban government on rightist groups with a long record of armed attacks on Cuba from US soil. "From start to finish," says the author, court proceedings were "tainted, corrupt, and vindictive. Every right to 'due process of law' was flouted." $22. Also in Spanish.

Pombo: A Man of Che's *guerrilla*

With Che Guevara in Bolivia, 1966–68

Harry Villegas

A firsthand account of the 1966–68 revolutionary campaign in Bolivia led by Ernesto Che Guevara. Under the nom de guerre Pombo, Harry Villegas, in his 20s at the time, was a member of Guevara's general staff. Villegas led the small group of combatants who survived the Bolivian army's encirclement and lived to recount this epic chapter in the history of the Americas. $23

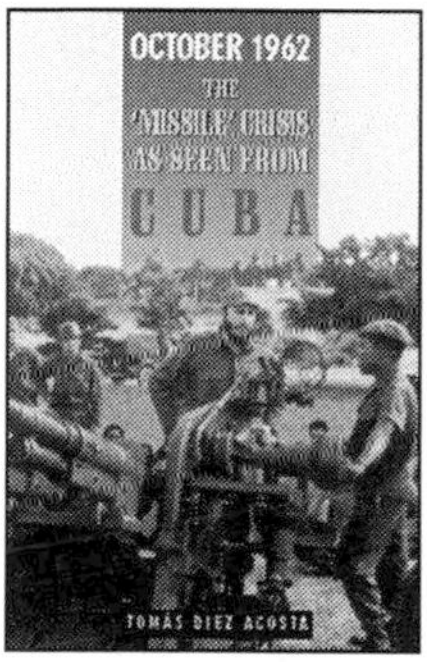

Dynamics of the Cuban Revolution

A Marxist Appreciation

Joseph Hansen

How did the Cuban Revolution unfold? Why does it represent an "unbearable challenge" to US imperialism? What political obstacles has it overcome? Written as the revolution advanced from its earliest days. $25

October 1962

The 'Missile' Crisis as Seen from Cuba

Tomás Diez Acosta

In October 1962 Washington pushed the world to the edge of nuclear war. Here the full story of that historic moment is told from the perspective of the Cuban people, whose determination to defend their sovereignty and their socialist revolution blocked US plans for a devastating military assault. $25

www.pathfinderpress.com

Basic works of

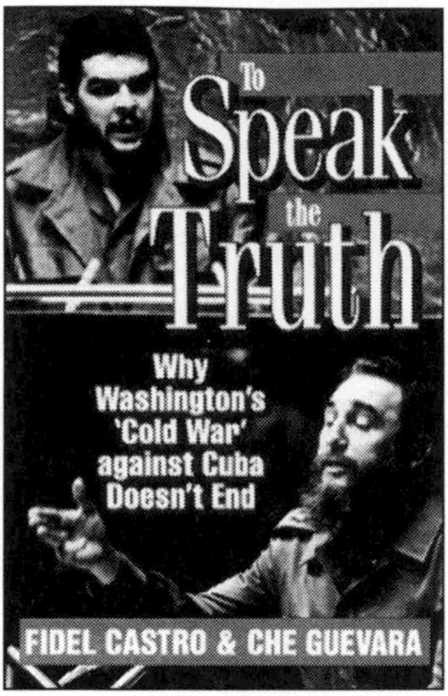

To Speak the Truth

Why Washington's 'Cold War' Against Cuba Doesn't End

Fidel Castro, Che Guevara

In historic speeches before the United Nations and UN bodies, Guevara and Castro address the peoples of the world, explaining why the US government so fears the example set by the socialist revolution in Cuba and why Washington's effort to destroy it will fail. $18

Che Guevara Talks to Young People

In eight talks from 1959 to 1964, the Argentine-born revolutionary challenges youth of Cuba and the world to study, to work, to become disciplined. To join the front lines of struggles, small and large. To politicize their organizations and themselves. To become a different kind of human being as they strive together with working people of all lands to transform the world. $15. Also in Spanish.

Episodes of the Cuban Revolutionary War, 1956–58

A firsthand account of the political events and military campaigns that culminated in the January 1959 popular insurrection that overthrew the US-backed dictatorship in Cuba. With clarity and humor, Guevara describes his own political education. He explains how the struggle transformed the men and women of the Rebel Army and July 26 Movement, opening the door to the first socialist revolution in the Americas. $30

Ernesto Che Guevara

Socialism and Man in Cuba

Guevara's best-known presentation of the political tasks and challenges in leading the transition from capitalism to socialism. Includes Fidel Castro's speech on the 20th anniversary of Guevara's death. Booklet. $7. Also in Spanish, French, Swedish and Farsi.

Che Guevara: Economics and Politics in the Transition to Socialism

Carlos Tablada

Quoting extensively from Guevara's writings and speeches on building socialism, this book presents the interrelationship of the market, economic planning, material incentives, and voluntary work; and why profit and other capitalist categories cannot be yardsticks for measuring progress in the transition to socialism. $21. Also in Spanish and French.

From the dictatorship of capital...

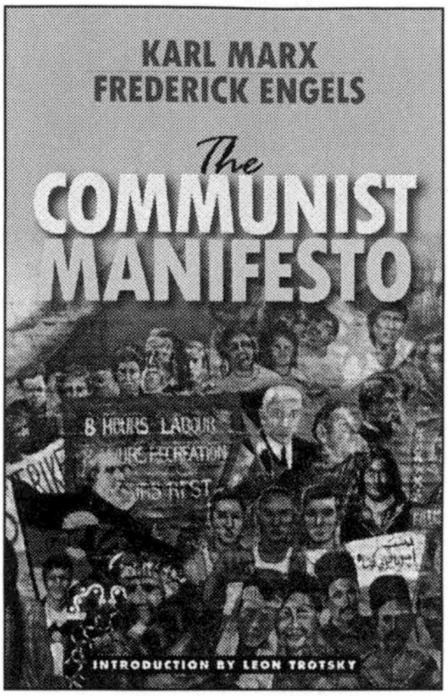

The Communist Manifesto

Karl Marx, Frederick Engels

Founding document of the modern revolutionary workers movement, published in 1848. Why communism is not a set of preconceived principles but the line of march of the working class toward power—a line of march "springing from an existing class struggle, a historical movement going on under our very eyes." $5. Also in Spanish, French, and Arabic.

State and Revolution

V.I. Lenin

"The relation of the socialist proletarian revolution to the state is acquiring not only practical political importance," wrote V.I. Lenin in this booklet just months before the October 1917 Russian Revolution. It also addresses the "most urgent problem of the day: explaining to the masses what they will have to do to free themselves from capitalist tyranny." In *Essential Works of Lenin.* $12.95

Their Trotsky and Ours

Jack Barnes

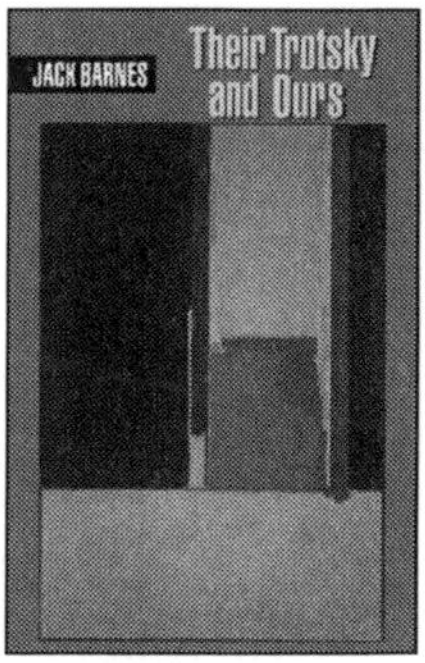

To lead the working class in a successful revolution, a mass proletarian party is needed whose cadres, well beforehand, have absorbed a world communist program, are proletarian in life and work, derive deep satisfaction from doing politics, and have forged a leadership with an acute sense of what to do next. This book is about building such a party. $16. Also in Spanish and French.

www.pathfinderpress.com

...to the dictatorship of the proletariat

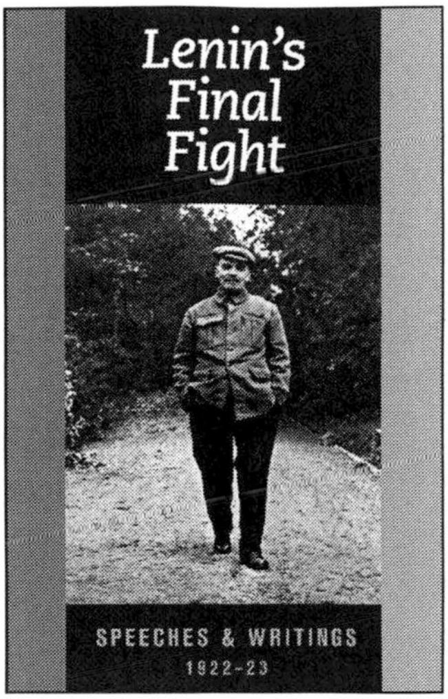

Lenin's Final Fight

Speeches and Writings, 1922–23

V.I. Lenin

In 1922 and 1923, V.I. Lenin, central leader of the world's first socialist revolution, waged what was to be his last political battle. At stake was whether that revolution would remain on the proletarian course that had brought workers and peasants to power in October 1917—and laid the foundations for a truly worldwide revolutionary movement of toilers organizing to emulate the Bolsheviks' example. $20. Also in Spanish.

Trade Unions: Their Past, Present, and Future

Karl Marx

Apart from being instruments "required for guerrilla fights between capital and labor," the unions "must now act deliberately as organizing centers of the working class in the broad interest of its complete emancipation," through revolutionary political action. Drafted by Marx for the First International's founding congress in 1866, this resolution appears in *Trade Unions in the Epoch of Imperialist Decay* by Leon Trotsky. $16

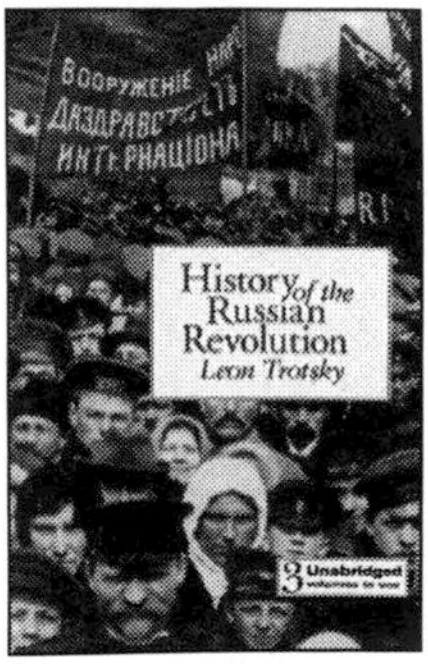

The History of the Russian Revolution

Leon Trotsky

The social, economic, and political dynamics of the first socialist revolution as told by one of its central leaders. How, under Lenin's leadership, the Bolshevik Party led the overturn of the monarchist regime of the landlords and capitalists and brought to power a government of the workers and peasants. Unabridged, 3 vols. in one. $38. Also in Russian.

New International

A MAGAZINE OF MARXIST POLITICS AND THEORY

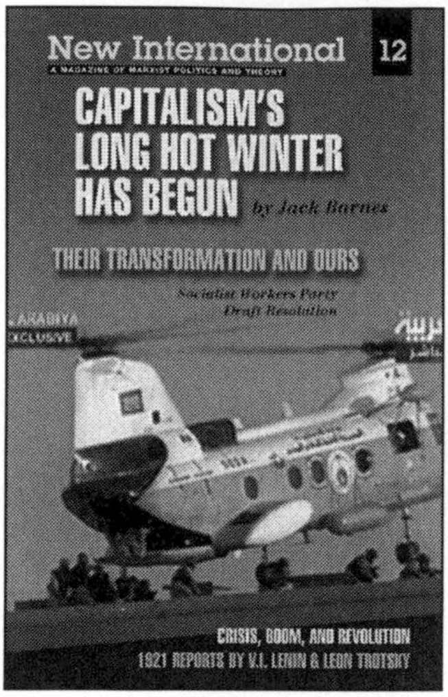

NEW INTERNATIONAL NO. 12

CAPITALISM'S LONG HOT WINTER HAS BEGUN

Jack Barnes

and "Their Transformation and Ours," Resolution of the Socialist Workers Party

Today's sharpening interimperialist conflicts are fueled both by the opening stages of what will be decades of economic, financial, and social convulsions and class battles, and by the most far-reaching shift in Washington's military policy and organization since the US buildup toward World War II. Class-struggle-minded working people must face this historic turning point for imperialism, and draw satisfaction from being "in their face" as we chart a revolutionary course to confront it. $16

NEW INTERNATIONAL NO. 13

OUR POLITICS START WITH THE WORLD

Jack Barnes

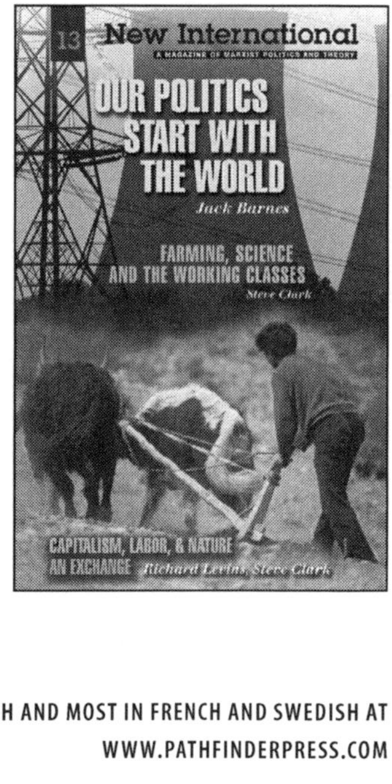

The huge economic and cultural inequalities between imperialist and semicolonial countries, and among classes within almost every country, are produced, reproduced, and accentuated by the workings of capitalism. For vanguard workers to build parties able to lead a successful revolutionary struggle for power in our own countries, says Jack Barnes in the lead article, our activity must be guided by a strategy to close this gap.

Also in No. 13: "Farming, Science, and the Working Classes" *by Steve Clark.* $14

THESE ISSUES ARE ALSO AVAILABLE IN SPANISH AND MOST IN FRENCH AND SWEDISH AT WWW.PATHFINDERPRESS.COM

NEW INTERNATIONAL NO. 11

U.S. Imperialism Has Lost the Cold War

Jack Barnes

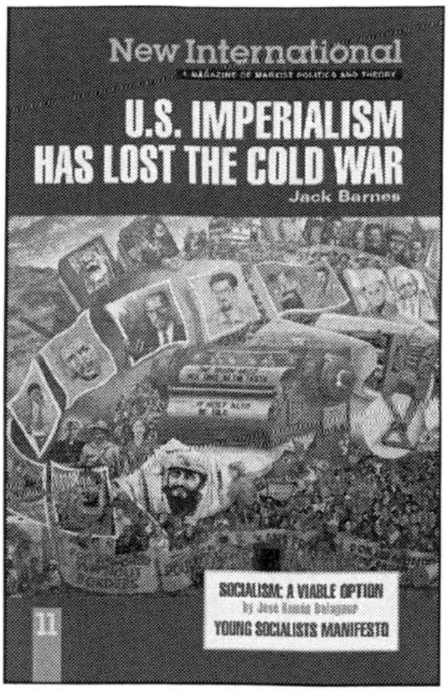

Contrary to imperialist expectations in the 1990s in the wake of the collapse of regimes across Eastern Europe and the USSR claiming to be communist, the workers and farmers there have not been crushed. The toilers remain an intractable obstacle to imperialism's advance, one the exploiters will have to confront in class battles and war. $16

NEW INTERNATIONAL NO. 8

Che Guevara, Cuba, and the Road to Socialism

Articles by Ernesto Che Guevara, Carlos Rafael Rodríguez, Carlos Tablada, Mary-Alice Waters, and Steve Clark and Jack Barnes

Exchanges from the opening years of the Cuban Revolution and today on the political perspectives defended by Guevara as he helped lead working people to advance the transformation of economic and social relations in Cuba. $10

IN NEW INTERNATIONAL NO. 10

Defending Cuba, Defending Cuba's Socialist Revolution

Mary-Alice Waters

In face of the greatest economic difficulties in the history of the revolution in the 1990s, Cuba's workers and farmers defended their political power, their independence and sovereignty, and the historic course they set out on at the opening of the 1960s. $16

EXPAND *Your Revolutionary Library*

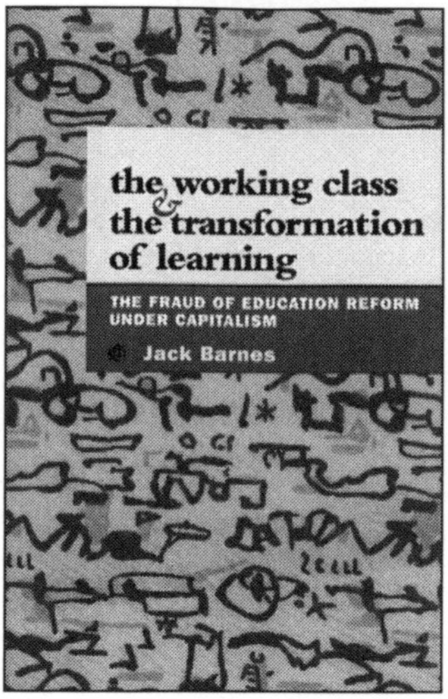

The Working Class and the Transformation of Learning

The Fraud of Education Reform under Capitalism

JACK BARNES

"Until society is reorganized so that education is a human activity from the time we are very young until the time we die, there will be no education worthy of working, creating humanity." $3. Also in Spanish, French, Swedish, Icelandic, Farsi, and Greek.

We Are Heirs of the World's Revolutions

Speeches from the Burkina Faso Revolution 1983–87

THOMAS SANKARA

How peasants and workers in this West African country established a popular revolutionary government and began to fight hunger, illiteracy and economic backwardness imposed by imperialist domination, and the oppression of women inherited from class society. They set an example not only for workers and small farmers in Africa, but those the world over. $10. Also in Spanish and French.

Problems of Women's Liberation

EVELYN REED

Six articles explore the social and economic roots of women's oppression from prehistoric society to modern capitalism and point the road forward to emancipation. $15

www.pathfinderpress.com

Malcolm X Talks to Young People

"You're living at a time of revolution," Malcolm told young people in the United Kingdom in December 1964. "And I for one will join in with anyone, I don't care what color you are, as long as you want to change the miserable condition that exists on this earth." Four talks and an interview given to young people in Ghana, the UK, and the United States in the last months of Malcolm's life. $15. Also in Spanish and French.

Capitalism and the Transformation of Africa

Reports from Equatorial Guinea

MARY-ALICE WATERS, MARTÍN KOPPEL

An account of the transformation of class relations in this Central African country, as it is drawn deeper into the world market and both a capitalist class and modern proletariat are born. The example of Cuba's socialist revolution comes alive in the collaboration of Cuban volunteer medical brigades there. Woven together, the outlines of a future to be fought for today can be seen—a future in which Africa's toilers have more weight in world politics than ever before. $10. Also in Spanish.

The Jewish Question

A Marxist Interpretation

ABRAM LEON

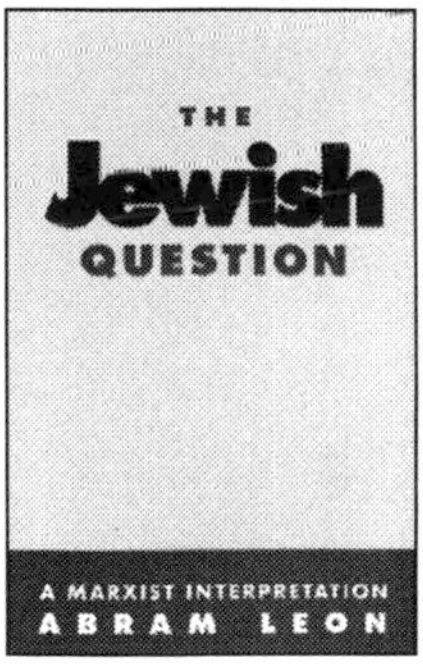

Traces the historical rationalizations of anti-Semitism to the fact that, in the centuries preceding the domination of industrial capitalism, Jews emerged as a "people-class" of merchants, moneylenders, and traders. Leon explains why the propertied rulers incite renewed Jew-hatred in the epoch of capitalism's decline. $22

PATHFINDER AROUND THE WORLD

Visit our website for a complete list of titles and to place orders

www.pathfinderpress.com

PATHFINDER DISTRIBUTORS

UNITED STATES

(and Caribbean, Latin America, and East Asia)

Pathfinder Books, 306 W. 37th St., 10th Floor,
New York, NY 10018

CANADA

Pathfinder Books, 7107 St. Denis, Suite 204,
Montreal, QC H2S 2S5

UNITED KINGDOM

(and Europe, Africa, Middle East, and South Asia)

Pathfinder Books, First Floor, 120 Bethnal Green Road
(entrance in Brick Lane), London E2 6DG

AUSTRALIA

(and Southeast Asia and the Pacific)

Pathfinder, Level 1, 3/281-287 Beamish St., Campsie, NSW 2194
Postal address: P.O. Box 164, Campsie, NSW 2194

NEW ZEALAND

Pathfinder, 4/125 Grafton Road, Grafton, Auckland
Postal address: P.O. Box 3025, Auckland 1140

Join the Pathfinder Readers Club
to get 15% discounts on all Pathfinder titles
and bigger discounts on special offers.
Sign up at www.pathfinderpress.com
or through the distributors above.